DEPRESSION

DEPRESSION

Self-Consciousness, Pretending, and Guilt

Ernest Keen

PRAEGER

Westport, Connecticut
London

Library of Congress Cataloging-in-Publication Data

Keen, Ernest, 1937–
  Depression : self-consciousness, pretending, and guilt / Ernest Keen.
    p. cm.
  Includes bibliographical references and index.
  ISBN 0–275–97567–3 (alk. paper)
  1. Depression, Mental. 2. Guilt. 3. Self-consciousness. I. Title.
RC537.K43 2002
  616.85′27—dc21   2001133081

British Library Cataloguing in Publication Data is available.

Library of Congress Catalog Card Number: 2001133081
ISBN: 0–275–97567–3

First published in 2002

Praeger Publishers, 88 Post Road West, Westport, CT 06881
An imprint of Greenwood Publishing Group, Inc.
www.praeger.com

Printed in the United States of America

The paper used in this book complies with the
Permanent Paper Standard issued by the National
Information Standards Organization (Z39.48–1984).

10 9 8 7 6 5 4 3 2 1

Contents

Contents

Prologue

There is no question that sadness is sometimes a complicated and fluid reaction to a loss—the death of someone close. Sadness is like standing in the waves. It is wet; it is cold. Sometimes it swamps you. Between such times it surrounds you; it slows you down and makes you realize your smallness, your weakness. It detaches you from what seem to be the trivial matters of rearranging your emotions, loyalties, and commitments, and from taking stock of what is left in order to join a future that re-engages the world.

It is probably equally beyond doubt that smaller losses, including seemingly trivial ones, can carry meanings so basic to one's life that it is like mourning a death in the family. Retirement, for example, is only partly a liberation. Once liberated, the emptiness can be more than disorienting; sometimes it is sad.

The recorded history of the human race is peppered with examples of mourning gone awry, and sadness thematizes a retreat into isolation, eccentricity, and madness. The modern period has tried to cope with this human phenomenon by cataloguing the extremes of sadness as a disease. Mourning is permitted, of course, and even elaborately ritualized, but nearly everyone's tolerance for the sadness of others is markedly limited. Most people who mourn feel alone, even in the presence of well-wishing family and friends.

Sadness, mourning, and struggle with loss are not medical matters, even when they disorient and confuse persons who suffer such difficulties. The intervention of doctors came about partly because the mental hospitals of the 19th century housed mourners who were overwhelmed, often permanently.

Further, the fact that all psychopathology engages one in loss has led us to confound normal and abnormal states and seems to lead to sadness that justifies depression as a psychiatric disease. Even genuine medical conditions are also occasions of loss, sadness, and struggle for a future. These struggles are not the medical conditions that occasion them, nor are they additional diseases that, like infections, are secondary to earlier diseases.

Nevertheless, the medical profession must deal with sadness and loss and inability to cope. The fact that doctors do so must be applauded. But any patient's resolve to cope with disease comes from some other quarter than the body of medical expertise. The mind is not the body, and it will not be reducible to the body even when (and if) we understand the brain. This sadness, and inability to deal with loss, is a different kind of failure from the body's failure to cope with infection or trauma—or with the normal bodily tasks of life.

Mental life, then, must be investigated in order to understand sadness and its struggle with the past and toward a future. At most, psychopharmacology can calm one's bodily cascades of endocrinological extremes, but if the problem is to be addressed, it is a mental struggle of the individual that addresses sadness about losses in the past and that faces the challenges of continuing life into a meaningful future.

Medicalization is a distraction from this task. It is actually a misdirection of effort. Rather than making a disease of sadness and tinkering with brain chemistry to address it, the person must become restored to a clarity of self and world that will enable the making of a future. Diagnosis of such well-known mental illnesses as depression are medicalized and ritualized in our culture and diagnoses can become a part of the problem instead of part of the solution. To cope with loss and sadness, and to reinvent the future, is task enough without the distractions of fearing depression, or worse. Further, even worse than fearing depression is our common tendency to enact depression as a script formulated in medical terms.

Aside from funerals, it is hard for a person to be sad in the presence of others without thinking of himself or herself as depressed, without distancing himself, as we all may do, by seeing a medical problem. In fact, sadness as my challenge becomes a more complicated dilemma because I know others will see me as depressed. In fact that complication divides my attention between my focus on self and future and my focus on how I appear to others.

In some, or perhaps all cases, part of the patient's depressive demeanor is a performance for others. This fact should surprise no one, for it is common that one's demeanor announces to others one's need to deal with sadness. If one is to do so, however, one should be in charge. However, the cultural tendency to see one's sadness as a disease encourages one to struggle with not only the interpersonal space one needs to regroup for the future, but to present a demeanor that justifies the special dispensations accorded one who is sick.

The medicalization of sadness into depression sometimes makes the second task, impression management, seem more urgent than the first task, groping for a future. To the extent this is true, all depression is both a genuine sadness and performance for others—both sadness and pretending to be depressed. I depend on the feedback from others to identify my own feelings, and this is always a greater factor than psychology takes into account.

I inevitably have difficulty telling my sadness from my pretending to be depressed. In fact, as author of my behavior, I cannot reliably separate the sadness I have from the sadness I enact for others. Even when I am alone, my emotional state coming from a loss and my emotional state enacted for others, become hopelessly intertwined and confused. In phenomenological terms, my "being in the world" and my "being for others" interpenetrate one another; the separate constituents become indivisible.

The main ideas for this book were formulated and delivered while I was a visiting lecturer in Psychology at Duquesne University's "Seminar in Contemporary Psychology" in the spring of 1984.

Introduction

The U.S. Public Health Service (hereafter cited as PHS, 1993) reports that one in eight individuals may require treatment for depression during his or her lifetime. Up to 70 percent of psychiatric hospitalizations were associated with mood disorders. The American Psychiatric Association (hereafter cited as APA, 1998) says that 15 percent of Americans will suffer major depression in their lifetimes, and another 5 percent will have less serious episodes.

According to the 1980 population base, the total number of cases of Major Depressive Disorder among those 18 or older in a six-month period was 4.8 million. In addition, over 60 percent of suicides have been attributed to Major Depressive Disorder (PHS, 1993). Of the generation born between 1940 and 1959, 10 percent have experienced an episode of depression by the age of 25, whereas the generation before that had a corresponding figure of only 2.5 percent (APA, 1998).

We can go on with such data about correlations and frequencies (such as the fact that women are twice or three times as frequently diagnosed), but at some point, we must ask if these data do not drive us to some other kind of conclusion. This book does not deny that depression happens. It hurts, and it is too frequent, but this book does suggest that there are more than medical facts here. There are also facts that are not medical but, rather, have to do with our concept of depression.

An undisputed authority such as T.B. Karasu (1990) is typical of the late 20th century in describing depression as a disease process, like cancer or tuberculosis—a natural event that befalls one from the fates, having only incidental connection to one's intentions. Even in his discussion of the interpersonal aspects of depression, four interpersonal situations are described as associated with major depression: (1) loss: prolonged grief reactions, (2) arguments: interpersonal role disputes, (3) change: difficult role transitions, and (4) failures: interpersonal deficits.

In thinking about Karasu's list, it seems empirically true that depression is most diagnosed when people fail to handle well such situations as these. Depression, it would seem, even complicates them. But what is depression apart from sadness in handling such situations badly? Sadness may follow failure, or sadness may come from somewhere else and cause failure. But where is the disease in such events? Except for the intervention of disease-naming professionals, it is, of course, the individual's struggles, not a disease, that is most central.

Such struggles as these can be dealt with by exploring the intentionalities enacted in these various situations. But in each, when depression as a disease becomes the focus of attention, we are steered away from the interpersonal dynamics that drive it and especially from the intentions that drive these relationships. Certainly there is little hint, in Karasu or other analysts, that either the client or therapist ought to take seriously the well-known script for enacting a posture of depression—a script that invites pretending. Such pretending is hardly limited to tactical or to situational maneuvers. It serves as a style of life—one that is lived as fully as a role, status, or even identity.

I am proposing that for some people, their sense of themselves and their appearance to others is not medical at all, that these facts are social and psychological. By using these terms, I mean to say not diseases in the usual sense. I am proposing that some large factor in these census data should be seen as a matter of pretending to be depressed.

Modern psychiatry conceives of depression as a spectrum disorder, meaning that it need not be a separate diagnosis, but rather one that spans the entire spectrum of pathology and health. This characterization helps us to avoid seeing depression as a disease and a cause, and it helps us to see it rather as something more basic to the intentional style of many individuals, regardless of diagnosis. In other words, if one is haunted by seemingly insuperable compulsions or obsessions, and one tries the entire repertoire of strategies for focusing on other things—living an ordinary life, even getting through a day without anxiety—and fails, of course one will be depressed—that is, feel discouraged, sad, guilty, and lonely.

Even when we see depression in such symptom pictures as biphasic mood shifts or chronic mild malaise (Akiskal, 1978), masked depression disguised as behavioral disturbances (Lesse, 1974), even difficult bereavement, it is not clear that we are dealing with a disease. To be sure, lithium, for example, evens out mood swings for bipolar patients. We do not know how it works except that it changes some physiology in the brain. This type of treatment, however, does not make moods into diseases. Alcohol and benzodiazapines also affect the brain to change moods, and we also do not know exactly how they work because we do not understand the brain in enough detail. Further, losses during infancy (Spitz, 1965), suicide in adolescence (Weiner, 1975), midlife crises (Levinson, 1978), and deteriorations of old age (Goldfarb, 1975) fall within what we have called, simply, depression. But these are not diseases; they are, perhaps, human tragedies or travails; they are difficult and people need help with them and manipulating brain chemistry can work.

But one depression is not like another, if one takes into account the life events that one is coping with. Losing a child is not like losing a parent or losing a job. A person in each of these situations may act similarly, but these life crises are not diseases; each person is struggling with tragedy, pain, loss—and each of these is unique. Does a single disease, called depression, underlie all these? Or are these phenomena better understood in their own right? Do they all simply express sadness? Or is what they express more particular than even that? In fact, it appears that entertaining even an intuitively valid common denominator risks falsifying the dynamics of particular situations. Calling depression a spectrum disorder is certainly an acceptable convention, but we see here also an intrusion of a disease label into places where other themes are more central.

The lesson from these comments should be to forget names of diseases and to work only descriptively to characterize and analyze the problems and experiences of people (Keen, 2000b). That people become sad in many ways makes sense and that they express their sadness in different ways makes sense. It even makes sense that their sadness interferes with the smoothness of their coping or their perspicacity in dealing with others.

It makes considerably less sense to explain the phenomena as caused by a disease called depression that appears as a spectrum disorder, even though Karasu supports his argument that depression underlies many states. He claims that support for the disease model lies in the traditional distinction between neurotic and normal depression, which can be seen in in the work of Sigmund Freud (1920). This claim is weak. Andreasen et al. (1980) also call attention to much confusion here. See also Sarbin and Keen (1997 and 1998).

Such a phrase as "pretending to be" makes the phenomenon sound childish, as in "let's pretend," which is not at all what I mean. Pretending is nothing more than what we all do everyday merely by the fact that we are intrinsically aware of being seen by others and that we cannot avoid knowing that. Thus, some aspects of our behavior are addressed to others as a coded communication. This involves psychology in a way different from the medical diagnosis and treatment of depression.

This study is a descriptive one that highlights how such phenomena as pretending and duplicity enter into our psychological lives so basically that visions of a disease called depression continually run amok. There is coherence in the theory presented here, but like other efforts to replace the medical model, this one is too partial to endure the long future course of straightening out all the conceptual confusion embedded in our thinking of depression as a disease. However, the theory presented here brings perspectives to bear that eventually must be included in our understanding of the life crises we now call depression.

This hypothesis asks us to understand the moodiness we call depression to be not a disease at all, but rather a social phenomenon, psychologically complex, to be sure, and worthy of attention. But the psychology of pretending to be depressed is hardly easy to get at. Most of all, we need to see pretending as not manipulative, exploitative, nor insincere. Rather it is simply how we all handle certain short-term situations and, in fewer cases, longer term situations—with longer-term patterns demanding personal or social recognition, not medical attention. They are not part of a medical problem, rather, they are part of a social one.

The ill-advised medicalization of social facts has been noted already, primarily by Thomas Szasz (1961, 1970, 1987). In the same way, the ill-advised prescription of psychiatric drugs has been explored by several investigators, such as Peter Breggin (1991), David Healy (1997), and Ernest Keen (1998, 2000a).

Amid the many critiques of the practice of medicalizing depression (e.g., Scull, 1989; Healy, 1997; Illich, 1976; Mirowsky and Ross, 1989; Sarbin, 1986; and Scheff, 1975), Karasu, a psychoanalyst (1990), points to the decisive critique that drugs could "destroy or reduce a crucial motivational source" for change. He goes on to say that"despite gradual modification of this view over the years, it is still believed that the major risk of administering pharmacologic agents during psychodynamic treatment is that the patient will use them as a crutch or substitute for introspection instead of relying on self-exploration" (p. 122). The danger, of course, threatens many more than those in psychodynamic treatment. Three-quarters of the anti-anxiety and anti-depressant medications (perhaps also even including antipsychotics) are prescribed by family physicians, not psychiatrists.

Thus, this book is a kind of specification and elaboration of Szasz's critique, but I hope that it is also an introduction to an approach in clinical psychology and psychiatry that can increasingly help us to understand what appears to us in the clinic. Such an understanding would suggest less pharmacological treatment and more psychological treatment. Such psychological treatment would involve a different approach than most current psychotherapies. Any elaboration of therapeutic technique requires further research and clinical experience, so it is too early to specify a technique. First, we have to understand the problem of depression differently.

Two additional facts should be noted. First, since the development of psychoactive drugs, the number of people who regularly use them to smooth out their adjustments to their jobs, families, and the tensions of reading the newspaper is many times the number of mental patients. As a population, are we happier, less depressed, more tranquil? Not visibly so. This means that beside those relatively few hospitalized patients for whom drugs have been decisive, the drug industry has roped in many tens of millions of people whose lives have rough edges and has made them patients, not in the major sense that being hospitalized makes a patient, but in the not insignificant sense that one is now under a doctor's care for one's nerves.

Second, attempting to control moods with chemicals is like trying to reprogram a computer with a screwdriver. The awesome power and complexity of the human brain far outstrips our understanding, and yet we seem to think that with a screwdriver we can start scratching the printed circuits in a computer and rearrange its functioning. If we find we can do about the same thing to its functioning every time with a particular scratch, should we then begin to feel that we are on the road to mastering its maddening tendency to do things we don't understand? Anyone with the least respect for the subtlety and intricacy of modern electronics would laugh at our hubris, our arrogance. Humility indeed is called for—an appreciation of the mystery and an attitude of respect before it—certainly not an aggressive marketing, multibillion dollar industry producing different kinds of screwdrivers.

It is hard to know whom to blame for our foibles here. Research should not stop, and drug industries support the research with at least some of their profits. General practitioners could be more discriminating in their prescription practices, as could psychiatrists, but the main problem seems to be ideological. As a culture, we believe in drugs the way we believe in good old American know-how. Further, we seem to be reassured when the loss or the struggle we endure is called a disease that has a treatment. But, what we really have to do about loss is learn to live without what was lost; what we have to do about failure is to keep trying instead of giving up; and what we have to do about our relationships is to take others seriously instead of parading about our own pain, guilt, sadness, and discouragement.

I certainly think that the treatment professions of psychiatry and clinical psychology can help with such matters, and in some cases, drugs seem to provide a breakthrough, but these facts do not make depression into a disease. The result of making depression into a disease is to arrange the legal and bureaucratic system so as to control antidepressant and other medicines—a difficult problem, given the fact that we can manipulate our moods and even thoughts with drugs.

The side effects of all this, however, are more than a dry mouth or sexual dysfunction or weight gain. It is to encourage pretending in a whole new way, not so we can enjoy drugs but so we can enact a role that is useful to us in some way. The roles of psychopathological states are well enough known that they increasingly populate our self-judgments—sometimes scaring us, of course. They also, however, populate the cast of characters from which we select our own lives.

CHAPTER ONE

Duplicity and Pretending

SINCERITY AND DUPLICITY

The behavior of a blue jay feeding on my back porch fascinates me. Cats also live here, and the jays have seen them many times. You can watch the jay check the environment carefully before committing itself to the vulnerability of eating. For only a second will the jay's attention be on the seed, perhaps much less than a second, and yet the jay watches, front and back, turns a little now to see the seed better, cocks its head a little more, then back to the original attitude, and finally, after much self-reassurance, the jay will eat.

This constant monitoring of the environment, visually and aurally, is a pattern selected through countless generations of pressure from predators. The blue jay has no choice in the matter; such paranoia is native and adaptive. Constant vigilance is the price of survival, and each posture, each repositioning of the body and head, is geared to a clearer and more complete watchfulness. The jay is aware—in the sense of being wary—of its environment. This awareness constantly seeks to detect the slightest motion or sound out of character amid the innocent rustling of leaves in the breeze.

The blue jay is also aware of other birds. It is accustomed to being left alone. The wrens and the sparrows leave when it arrives. If a sparrow seems to hang back, the jay flutters its wings slightly, and the sparrow departs. The jay is also aware of the kinds of seed available. The large, black ones are not its choice; it looks for the small yellow ones—will they be there? Or will there be only yesterday's husks? The jay knows in an instant and behaves accordingly.

My own reputation with the jays is mixed. I'm often allowed to move around at some distance but not always. On some days, the jay seems intolerant of even a slow and clumsy human. At other times, I can come much closer than any cat is allowed before the jay leaves for a nearby limb, to watch me pass by, so that it can return.

So the awareness of the blue jay is far from limited to cats and other dangers. It is also attuned to its colleagues, to the kinds and availability of food, even to whether I am just passing by so it can return to the feeder. This jay's world is complex, spatially and temporally. I can come much closer than a cat before the jay will leave. This fact suggests that the jay may be sensitive to possible futures by watching current events.

The blue jay may not know that I cannot traverse six feet in a second and that my cat can; it may not formulate "clumsy human" and "svelte cat," or even "slow" and "fast" at all, but its sense of the world is accurate. The presence of another bird or a colored seed is meaningful to the jay, as it forages its way through the day, negotiating the scores and hundreds and thousands of cues to which it has ready responses.

As the blue jay attends to me, the sky, the seed, another bird, in back of itself, to the sky again, it is totally absorbed in its world. Human beings are rarely like this for more than a few minutes. Such concentration is broken by another awareness, an awareness of one*self*, a self-consciousness that can be delayed only for a few minutes in humans and then only if a task is absorbing.

But I cannot, like the blue jay, move from task, to danger, to opportunity, seriatim, without moments of self-consciousness. "Should I take a break? No, stay with it. But I'm tired. But it has to get done." Such unspoken chatter punctuates my concentration in a way we suppose is quite foreign to the jay's awareness. Were the jay as distractible from its absorption in the world, it would lapse its vigilance, and it would become vulnerable.

To be sure, the blue jay is distracted from the eating task, but not in the way I am likely to wander away from the world before me, thinking of idle events of the day as if they mattered, totally losing track of the sequence of words my eyes dutifully keep scanning. If the jay had my consciousness, my cat would have the jay.

Not only would my consciousness be quite inadequate to the jay's life and world, but the jay's awareness is insufficient for mine. That extra layer of consciousness[1] makes my paranoia more complex. "What will they think if I don't get it done? But there's still time for a snack. Am I really hungry?" Alongside my fatigue and hunger is an ever-present sense of what "they" will think.

Does the jay wonder what the wren, or the cat, thinks? Probably not. Seeing myself imaginatively through the eyes of others is probably a uniquely human activity; it is quite superfluous to the blue jay and would, in fact, unnecessarily complicate and make inefficient its existing system of staying out of trouble.

Human beings, however, are native egoists; we think of ourselves, inevitably and more or less constantly. This second layer of consciousness shares the stage with our awareness of the world. I, too, can be wary of my environment, and like the jay, I can proceed through a dark alley with alert caution, but it takes effort—effort to turn off reflection, to turn off wondering what "they'll" think if "they" see my caution, or find me dead in the alley, and so forth..

Most of the time I do not put out that effort, and so my ordinary day is negotiated by a double consciousness of the world, and of myself, or of the world and of myself as seeing the world, or of the world as I see it versus the world as I think someone else sees it. Fond as I am of my blue jays, I must leave them behind now and introduce the complexities born of this double consciousness.[2]

This double consciousness is complex, but not usually as complex as it might be. My second consciousness— my self-consciousness—is not free to roam the world of my perception, finding and playing with images and nuances. My self-consciousness is quite thoroughly socialized. It has themes and formats and patterns that are enormously redundant and repetitive. It is effortless to let my perceptual awareness of the world follow the world's lead into whatever strikes me as interesting. There is always something interesting in the world to pursue. In order to enjoy the same freedom in my self-consciousness, I must put out effort—and I usually do not— to think reflectively about myself.

Particularly rare, in reflection as well as in merely observing the world, is thinking in ways other than those dictated by my particular social group. So that even if I do scan myself with the kind of curiosity that I scan the environment, I find less variety. In William James's terms, "Here I am, the same old me again." I really am more easily bored with myself than with the world. Those of us who are not are often diagnosed as psychopathological. Nevertheless, my second consciousness does open up mental and social possibilities to me that are forever denied the blue jay. The mental possibilities, while striking, are not frequently actualized by most humans. They include examining my own thoughts from a point of view detached from that point of view of the thoughts themselves. Such reflective self-scrutiny is a splendid way to detect the limits and biases of my own perspective. It is rarely used by me and others like me; most human beings don't bother with it at all.

At some time or another, almost all human beings do, at least for a short time, exercise the liberating possibilities of the second consciousness. For example, if I continue to misjudge my opponent's tennis serve, or my son's motives, I may note these errors and reflectively ask why I am making them. Such inquiry may reveal that my opponent's body language or my son's contemptuous sneer was causing me to jump to untrue conclusions. This causal relationship was in effect until I became conscious of it. Once I am conscious of it, I am no longer subject to its influence in the same way; I am liberated from that cause; I have become more free than I formerly had been—free to see and to say things formerly impossible for me.

But while such liberation is possible, most human beings do not often take advantage of it. A much more common and—as we shall see in chapter 5—more momentous possibility is opened up because my second consciousness is infiltrated and permeated by cultural content. I refer to the ability to imagine versions of reality that are not real but could be.

I envision a perfect society, a perfect me, a perfect nine-iron shot out of a sand trap. Such imaginings, plus the possibility that I could try to make them real, are basic to morality. Morality is an intensely social and personal matter of great psychological importance, as we shall presently see. Less statuesquely, but no less importantly, stands my ability, advanced far beyond that of the blue jay, to engage a species mate in a shared topic of concern. I can engage in conversations. Have I ever said anything to anyone without "hearing" my remark from the other's point of view—or from what I think is the other's point of view?

I have surely failed to take my listener seriously and misjudged what he or she would think, but I did not speak without my self-consciousness telling me how I thought it was being heard by another in his or her consciousness of me. Indeed, human beings deal with other human beings in linguistic codes of such sophistication and refinement that it is impossible to have a conversation without hearing one's own speech from the other's point of view.

That hearing is, after all, how I know what to say in order to be understood. It is as native to me as the blue jay's wariness, and it creates a paranoia, as I've said, more complex than that of the jay. Speaking involves hearing myself from your point of view. Speaking is a social activity and depends on such self-consciousness. Animals, who do not speak as we do, do not need self-consciousness in order to sustain their sociality. But speaking is not the only social activity of humans. In one sense, all human activity is social. Like speaking, it is accompanied by that second, self-consciousness. My activity, like my speaking, is implicitly but constantly being "heard" by me from the point of view of the other to whom I am speaking.

When I am alone, such fantasies of how I would look to others, such self-consciousness, is akin to noise; it interferes with my concentration on a task. It is unwanted and not useful but is nevertheless present, at least in spurts if not more or less constantly. In that sense, all behavior, no matter how solitary, when enacted by human beings, is inescapably social, even though the "other" may be absent or a mere fantasy.

Even if my consciousness of myself with another has atrophied into an unspoken conversation with myself, the self to whom I speak is a listener like another and, in my fantasy, becomes also a speaker. Both speaker and listener, the dialogue, and the sociality can be played out by me alone—a uniquely human event that requires a consciousness, plus a second consciousness to be conscious of the first, plus a rich catalogue of others whose internal complexity matches my own. All of this is native to a single consciousness of a human being.

Most of the time, the doubleness in consciousness when I speak reduces to the relatively simple format of a simultaneous consciousness of my own intended comment, and of your ability to hear it. Even so, there are, of course, many more layers to consciousness during speech, such as remembering what I said yesterday or heard the day before and what you might think later of me or whether I will know what you think, and so on. But the doubleness is basic and always there. It is inherent in speech behavior that both speaker and listener are conscious of both speaker and listener—as points of view. As I write this, I also read it from the point of view of an anonymous reader. That is how I know what to write. It is like a conversation, where both parties enact their own role while covertly imagining the other. But right now, of course, as I write, it is all simply in my own consciousness.

The second consciousness, in myself and in everyone, then, is very busy, bound to its task much more tightly than is my simple perception of the world. I can look at anything, but my second consciousness is preoccupied with themes of myself and how I look in your eyes, according to prescribed criteria. Even when there is no one else to pay attention to, or to pay attention to me, my second consciousness does not totally, or for long recede, but returns or continues its activities, clumsily inventing another, or pretending one is there, continuing its second-order monitoring of my behavior in apparently useless but inevitable ways.

My everyday behavior engages this doubleness with as much native ease as the blue jay watches behind itself. That means that I never do anything as unequivocally as the blue jay. My behavior is always double, duplicitous, enacting a motive of my own, for my own reasons, and enacting a drama for the other to see. I am often just as conscious of the second as I am of the first. My motives, therefore, are always mixed. I do what I do for the reasons I say, but also for its appearance to another. There are really very few exceptions to this generalization—limited to reflex or impulsive behavior, or that relatively rare behavior executed while totally concentrating on just what is in front of me.

In light of this normal duplicity, it is curious that we should put such a premium on so-called sincere behavior. Sincere behavior is behavior I "really mean" as opposed to things done or said for their effect on another. But almost all behavior is both. Duplicity is inevitable. In speaking (and it is no different with most things I do), I not only say what I think, I am simultaneously aware of how you will hear what I say, and what you will think of it. I therefore nudge my saying this way or that so as to maximize its effect on you. Human speech, in this sense, is inherently more complex than simply sincerity. So is most human behavior.

In order for my point to be impossible to miss, I should move, from speech and my decisions about how to say things in light of your hearing, to my way of being a person and my decisions about how to live in light of your perception of me. "How to be a person" is nothing more than an extended version of "how to handle a situation." I often ask others or myself how I should handle a situation, enacting my second consciousness of others' reactions in order to guide just how to express my first (sincere) consciousness of the situation. If the duplicity of such situation handling is clear, it is a short step to seeing that life is just a rather larger situation, which I handle by being myself, and that being myself is duplicitous, simultaneously oriented to what and who I want to be and to what and who I want you to think I am. I am both sincere—and not; I express my reaction to the world, and I gauge that expression to what I think you'll think of me. I am who I want to be *and* I am in such a way as to impress you about who I am or want to be. This duplicity in my behavior is inevitable—as it is in your behavior; as it is in so-called psychopathology. That is the point. Abnormal behavior, like all human behavior, is duplicitous and that duplicity must be understood before we can answer such questions as we might have about it, including its psychopathology.

To say that most pathological behavior is duplicitous is not to pronounce a judgment on its insincerity, but rather it is to point to its similarity to nonpathological behavior, to its orientation to observers' judgments, through prescribed criteria that are well known to us all. To say that pathology is duplicitous is to highlight a way pathology may deceive us. But it is also to point to how pathology is therefore at the same time a condition that is like nonpathological behavior, and it is to suggest, finally, that the most serious pathologies are exactly those that have lost their duplicity.

CHARACTER AND CULTURE

What are the prescribed criteria that are well known to all of us—of which I spoke above? Norms, roles, values, rules, mores—each of these names an aspect or level of such criteria of social judgment. They are part of our culture—that thick matrix of matrices that gives birth to social meaning in our very complex everyday experience.

One can also point, as I did before, to themes, formats, and patterns that preoccupy my self-consciousness and dictate what questions to ask about myself because others are answering them about me and I want their answers to be of some particular character.

Let us move, for a moment, from concepts to character, beginning with a concrete character.

Chip's Story

We called him Chip, and I don't think any of us at the university knew his real name, or cared. He delivered our *New York Times* to us loyally, and he would occasionally stop to chat about the weather or his church's sale of peanut brittle. Chip may have been retarded, or perhaps he was simply uneducated—so uneducated that he didn't know not to speak to professors as if they were equals. He wore second-hand clothes, but occasionally had a new scarf or new gloves. I recall particularly the day he sported a new hat, telling me proudly that he bought it.

At any rate, we indulged and pampered him, thinking of him almost as a pet, certainly as a child, even as he passed into his seventh decade. I suppose he enjoyed his contact with professors, condescending and paternalistic though we were. Then about 10 years ago, he just disappeared. Where did he go? Is he still alive? I don't know. It is noteworthy that as important as Chip became to us, we really treated him with un-conscionable condescension. I am ashamed that I do not even know what happened to him.

But Chip is memorable not only because he was willing to be the "town character"—just a step away from "court jester" or "village fool." He is memorable because he had a distinct sense of how a man is supposed to be, and he never wavered in the slightest from his consci-entious carrying out of his assigned task of paper delivery, his scrupu-lous honesty with money, his obligation to sell peanut brittle for his church, and so on. Not a complex man, Chip nevertheless must be called a good man; he certainly worked harder at being a good man than many good men I know and respect.

Chip knew the prescribed criteria of being a good man, in spite of his retardation and/or his lack of education. He was a cultured man, in that sense, as we all are. His self-consciousness was populated with criteria of self-judgment that enabled him to stay out of trouble as surely as we all do, or as surely as the the blue jay stays out of trouble without them.

Chip's environment is the human, social world, and his second layer of consciousness guided his behavior successfully through a labyrinth of social judgments. Of course Chip's behavior was much more com-plex than that of the blue jay, but like all human behavior, it was as effi-cient as the blue jay's alert wariness, which guided it through day after day of foraging.

Chip handled the situation of life by enacting a self that he called a good man, and a self that he was relatively sure others would similarly judge. He may or may not have heard of a court jester, but he had a sense that there was a place for him, even as a 60–year-old paper boy, as long as he retained the good will of professors and others who were ob-viously of a higher social rank. He was, therefore, both sincere and du-plicitous. He showed us both who he really was and who he wanted us to see.

Our culture, in its density, has a variety of characters already estab-lished. They are like types of people. Each of us has a unique list of types of people we know and recognize, but our lists are also somewhat alike. Those commonalities are one version of the culture's cast of characters (Scheib, 1995). In being who we are, we enact one or some combina-tion of just these types, and we know that others will see us as one or some combination. We worry if we are perceived very differently from how we want to be perceived. Nothing is more uncomfortable, for in such cases, the second layer of consciousness is failing to guide our be-havior so as to create the impression we want to create.

As mentioned, embedded in these characters, or types, are our categories of psychopathology. However, perhaps it is more accurate to say that our diagnostic catalogue is some version of pre-existing cultural types. At any rate, no one is pathological, no one is neurotic, psychotic, or disturbed or has an emotional illness without the second consciousness telling him who he or she is being for others.

I recall the many trips to Danville State Hospital with my students in Abnormal Psychology, where we spent an evening a week in "Just for Fun Classes"—games, crafts, discussions. Patients there nearly always made a point of telling the students that they knew they were mental patients. In the rare case that a patient did not have an awareness of that role, a nurse nearby always watched to make sure that his or her lack of that second consciousness did not lead to some bizarre or potentially frightening behavior. However, in the years that I was involved there, that never happened.

Escaping such an awareness is very rare. Ironically, it is rare also in psychopathology, even though it is clearly psychopathological to not be aware in this way. That is, some paranoid persons do not simply enact a role of paranoid; for them, the world is transformed into a dangerous place, and they misjudge how they are seen by others.

At the same time, there is no escaping the conclusion that those of us who "adopt the patient role," as we say, are opting for a particular way of handling the situation of life. When the paranoid "knows" he is paranoid and begins hiding his suspiciousness and courageously letting people be near him without fearing them, we think he is improving. This handling of social contact by mental patients is no more or less duplicitous than other ways of life.

People, therefore, pretend all the time, often even in their pathology. Let us explore other ways in which we pretend, ways that we create an impression of one thing while perhaps hiding exactly the opposite, or ways in which we play at being a certain way, sometimes for a short while, sometimes only in certain settings, and so on.

PRETENDING AND CULTURE

People pretend within a complex network of myths, meanings, agreements and understandings that control their pretending and give them something to pretend about. All behavior occurs within this dense thicket of prior and evolving shared agreements, most of which are unspoken, some of which are unspeakable. Pretending, like any behavior, must be analyzed in this context. For example, suppose you

could spy on my dinner table and saw my daughter and me having a dis-
agreement about whether she will watch television after supper. She
says things such as "You never let me do what I want to do." "You
don't understand anything." "You won't be able to control my life after
I leave this house." I respond by saying things such as "Television will
rot your brain." "Maybe you don't like homework, but that's all the
more reason to have the discipline to do it." "One of these days you'll
see I was right all along."

This conversation could appear (probably already has appeared) on
television. Fathers and daughters have these kinds of conversations in
our society. You, the spy, however, do not know, without knowing my
daughter and me, just what the fight is really about. It could be about:

1. whether she shall watch television after supper
2. whether father or daughter has the authority to make such decisions about
   such things
3. whether father loves daughter and daughter loves father
4. whether father or daughter shall survive as a person, which is possible only
   at the expense of the survival of the other.

If the fight is about (1) whether my daughter will watch television,
then issues (2), (3), and (4) are more or less tacitly agreed upon and not
at issue. My authority is not really at stake, nor is her power to affect it;
we both agree that I have a certain amount of power and she has a certain amount, and we are not defending our power nor do we feel that it
is in danger or that either of us is in danger of losing a grip on "self."

The fight takes place within a set of agreements that not much is really at stake here. The fight is really about tonight. We both somehow
understand that power and authority, who loves whom, or who survives, is not at risk even though our histrionics may try to intimidate
one another by parading such an issue. This would be pretending. "You
aren't a father at all; you're a petty tyrant." "If you flunk English, you're
no daughter of mine."

If issue (2), who has the authority, father or daughter, to decide
about daughter's behavior, is at stake, then the television that evening is
merely symbolic of the more central power issue. Issues (3) and (4),
however, are still agreed upon and are not at stake. It is culturally approved, through the notion of the "generation gap," that fathers and
daughters are supposed to contend this, and that contention can be
quite serious without risking their agreements about who loves whom
or who will be allowed to survive in his or her identity as a person.

If the fight is about (3), the testing of love, then it is more serious and more central to each party, and TV watching and even authority are mere symbols. This more serious fight about love, however, may (and usually does) take place against the backdrop of an agreement about (4). Neither has to annihilate the other in order to survive. This third level of meaning may be less common in such scenes, and we wonder in such cases what has happened to the culturally prescribed pattern of who is obliged to love whom and under what conditions such love can be withdrawn, conditional, or tentative.

If the fight is really about (4), then each party has really become so serious that tragedy is inevitable. Father, in order to sustain his sense of his own identity, *must* make his daughter prove her love, by granting him authority to tell her not to watch television. The daughter, in order merely to survive, must make father prove his love, by granting her the freedom to watch television. The symbols symbolize progressively larger stakes; the background of agreement that hosts and limits the argument gets progressively smaller, then nonexistent. Sometimes, everything *is* at stake.

Real conflicts that are this serious, with this little supporting common ground or agreement, are relatively rare within families, although they are common between cultures. Warfare is their explicit enactment. In the 20th century (and it has not always been so, but it is also not unique to the 20th century), we saw so-called total war, where no common agreement hosted the conflict, and there was no guarantee that any persons or groups would survive. There were, therefore, no rules. The rules, the culture itself, was at stake and ceased being a framework within which the interaction took place.

It is interesting to note that the warfare of the United States since World War II has not been at this level of seriousness, even though many lives have been lost. Again, our recent wars are not unique in the history of humankind, but we have reversed things in a curious way so that the ultimate stakes (life, survival) have become mere symbols, and the more superficial, symbolic issues (prestige, credibility, and hegemony, markets, and profits) have become the point of going to war.

In families, as opposed to battlefields, this hierarchy of issues is usually agreed upon, and while it may take a while for contestants to understand exactly how much the other has at stake, there is almost always an agreement that both can survive, and a good deal more agreement as well. I recall, however, a family in which the fight was really about (4). Both father and daughter tried to let the other know that "I really mean it," just as my daughter and I do. When my daughter and I do that, however, we don't really mean that our survival is at stake, even though we may pretend it is. "If you flunk Math, you can move to an apartment and buy your own TV set." "You'll be sorry if you don't ever see me again!"

This pretending is in the service of settling a more superficial issue like authority or love. It is not a serious threat of annihilation, or even abandonment, and fathers and daughters usually know it. My daughter and I may pretend that survival is at stake in the TV decision. But when the issue really *is* survival, when each puts everything on the line, then the pretending goes the other way. Such people might be pretending that TV watching is at stake when really their personal survival is at stake. They are then pretending to be only pretending that it is a life-or-death issue. Unfortunately, it is.

This network of agreements, laid out hierarchically, within which people pretend, is really part of the complex matrix of culture. Enacting disagreements at various levels at various times in order to settle various issues, such as the inevitable power-authority issue, or the crucial issue of love, is already prescribed, and these arguments have the flavor of ritual. Rituals are vital to the maintenance of the agreements, and yet they are not allowed to be called merely rituals or else they'd lose their effectiveness not only in settling important questions, but, more basically, in affirming that certain *other* questions are *not* at stake.

The pretending described in this book is within the cultural matrix even as it is about the cultural matrix, or about how you and I shall enact it. If we grow up in families, we grow up in culture, and if we grow up in culture, we enact prescribed rituals that develop, refine, and affirm the cultural matrix. Pretending, like duplicity, is thus inevitable and reflects, in one sense, nothing more surprising than the multiplicity of reference in all human articulation.

Is there a qualitative difference between the pretending by my daughter and myself, on the one hand, and pretending in psychopathology on the other? The former pretending is ritualistic, and many people are included in the ritual, in the framework of agreements within which the ritual works to settle some things and affirm other things. The other people implicitly know what is going on, and they play their reciprocal parts. Surprises are clearly constrained by the fact that only certain things are at stake while other things definitely are not, and everyone (implicitly) knows it.

Abnormal pretending differs from this inevitable pretending by not being a part of a ritual and, hence, not being intelligible to others. In psychopathology, the stakes of controversies become ambiguous; one does not know, and cannot get a sense of, what agreements are safe and what ones are in question.

In psychopathology, the agreements that frame conflicts are notable in their absence. Some years ago, I inadvertently backed into the car behind me as I was leaving a parking place. The owner of the other car was just walking by, and he saw my bumper go above his and dent his car's hood. As I was getting out of my car to leave him a note, he rushed up to me and threatened to "waste" me right then and there.

Was he kidding? Was he exaggerating in a way permitted when one's car is damaged? In my scale of values, a dented hood is not worth a human life but was that true for him? For a moment, I thought he meant it, and maybe he did, for a moment, until he caught himself and refrained from following through.

The culture reinstituted itself; his threat (if it was serious) became ritual, and he did not need to be embarrassed by it. He could claim, implicitly, to be pretending in that ordinary and expected way that accompanies ritual and culture, but for a moment I was frightened. I wondered if my insult to his car suddenly became a life and death matter. If he had identified with his car in a certain way—say, he saw his car's perfection as the purity of his own virtue and every scratch as a rape, against which unlimited righteous indignation is justifiable. If that had been his way of being in the world, then his ritual was private and not cultural.

In that case, it would not have been intelligible to me why he was about to kill me. The background agreement, against which we both could count on some things not being at stake, would have been absent. As I mentioned, when he threatened to "waste me," the thought crossed my mind that he meant it. Fortunately, the culture's prescription for pretending was in effect rather than his true intentions.

Soon we shall be considering depression, and pretending to be depressed. Pretending to be depressed is like the case of denting the man's hood in that there was ambiguity of the stakes of controversy. I did not know him, so I had no real clarity about the background agreements he subscribed to. It was just possible that a hood is worth exactly one life. But he was, in fact just pretending. Pretending to be depressed is pretending that a life and death issue is afoot when it is not.

We need now to clear up what is and what is not a life and death issue. When a father needs his daughter to prove her love, by granting him authority, by not watching TV, he may need it as reassurance that he is who he thinks he is, or he may need it in order to continue feeling as though he is anyone at all, a valid human being. Real desperation along these lines is far from unheard of, and fathers like this tend to have daughters whose needs are equally desperate, inevitably creating tragedy. Someone has to lose. But what would losing mean? Father may not be able to sustain the coherence of his life without his daughter's acquiescence. He may "decompensate," "go berserk," or become so desperate that he actually kills or maims or so panicked that he withdraws in terror and becomes catatonic.

His daughter's hold on a personal identity may as well be very shaky; she may lose not only a night's TV watching but also her last remnant of hope that she will ever be able to stand on her own two feet and face life without cringing and stuttering and eventually collapsing into incoherent sobs—an increasingly frequent and potentially typical way for her to handle life.

For people who have these kinds of things at stake all the time, there is only tragedy. Life and death are not biologically at stake, but psychologically putting them at stake symbolically is an interpersonal strategy that is dangerous. The person who blackmails another with a suicide threat, or gets his way with a threat of murder, is playing a dangerous game. We actually weaken our stance in life, or our status as a person, by threatening to raise the stakes in this way. Life's resulting poker game can lead to a called bluff, or a called nonbluff, and someone will lose. A collapse is possible, and like in poker, some collapses leave us crippled in our ability to rejoin the fray. Some threats and bluffs lead to a crippling that leads us in turn to real failures in the difficult matter of living.

Depression is also a life and death matter. Giving up is a continual human possibility. We know of giving up as a possibility because we've done it, albeit on a small scale, and we certainly know of depression as a kind of pathology, as a role, and as a set of excuses that make it unnecessary to meet the usual rigors of life.

We know of suicide, too. To get depressed is often, but not always, pretending to give up. To be sure, going berserk in a panic is sometimes pretending to be at the edge of ultimate stakes as well, but pretending to go berserk, when there really are other ways available to handle a situation, is rare. Pretending to get depressed is not.

SUMMARY

We began by describing the awareness of my blue jay and the contrasting second consciousness of human beings. That second consciousness makes possible self-criticism, even liberation from certain causalities in our lives, but it is more usually simply the consciousness of ourselves in another's eyes. Such awareness of ourselves in another's eyes gives all our behavior a kind of duplicity, a doubleness of motive in which we do what we want to do *and* we create the impression we want to create.

The existence of the second, impression-creating motive makes our behavior almost always something other than sincere—something more and more complex. Weaving its way through this complexity are the themes of our culture, which include standards of judgment that we know we all have, and hierarchies of agreement within which our disagreements are enacted.

Cultural frames contain controversy, except in those extraordinary situations where everything comes to be at stake at once. Most controversies are not so serious, although the contestants are permitted or even expected to pretend that they are. Such pretending, like the duplicity born of self-consciousness, is at once insincere but quite inevitable, certainly necessary, and even irreplaceably useful in the workings of social life.

The culture also contains a stock of characters—the village idiot, the pillar of the community, and so on. In recent times, psychological-diagnostic types have become common members of our cast of characters. These characters, too, are part of our second consciousness—we wonder if we fulfill the one in another's eyes that we want to fulfill.

After this initial foray into the complexity and intricacy of duplicity and pretending, we need to pay particular attention to another complexity, that of human volition, to which we now turn.

CHAPTER TWO

Volition

GOING BERSERK

There is a facticity, a concreteness, about the rhythms of my body, its responses, its explosions, certainly its desires. In some situations, I can feel my body respond. The responses seem independent of me in that they are not willed. Their momentum is given. William James (1890) referred to this experience as one of "an automaton." We are all automatons, James argues, unless we actively intervene. Our passivity—our passive acceptance of an automatic behavior—may result in our being very active indeed, as in an explosion of anger. Put another way, active angry explosions are, in an important sense, passive. We give in to their automaticity.

In contrast, my active willing to get angry is notable in its affective failure. In order for me to succeed in getting angry, I must do more than decide to get angry. I must be in the presence of angering stimuli, either physical or imaginary. Some people carry around a repertoire of imaginative angering situations and call upon them from time to time in order to get angry when they want to. Fearing I will be intimidated in a confrontation with my boss, I tell myself to remember how he deceived me here and slighted me there. This self-coaching is really an effort to mobilize the automaticity of anger, which in turn is necessary because I cannot quite do it by merely deciding to. Anger is not a matter of fiat.

Why is this so? Anger is usually thought of as a loss of control, while decisions and fiats are considered control. It is impossible for control to simply abandon itself and at the same time determine what will result. I must, therefore, not only willingly abandon control, I must give control over to particular stimuli that I know will make me angry. If I give up control without giving control over to such an automatism I can predict, then anything may result. I may go to sleep, laugh, or sink into a dumb emptiness. It is, therefore, possible to decide to get angry, but only if I can summon up those cues that mobilize my anger and only if I can give myself over to them. In the face of an angering situation, on the other hand, getting angry is much less complex; I need only to give in to a bodily pattern already under way.

"To give in to . . ." This phrase covers more than a single phenomenon. My anger may explode without my awareness of a choice to give in to it or not. On one hand, it may well up in my stomach, and I can chose to express it or not. On the other hand, its welling may so overwhelm me that I cannot be pleasant; the best I can do is to be silent. Every concrete instance is a little different in terms of the time relations—when I feel the anger; when I lose control; when I am conscious of an option to block, if not conceal, my reaction, or even to stop it outright, count to ten, then look at the situation again.

Anger outbursts are usually fairly short affairs. They lead rather quickly into a post-anger period when I will have to live with the fact that I got angry. However, getting angry, either automatically or by giving in to it, rarely aims at a future post-anger situation that is considered ahead of time. Anger is rarely, in other words, a calculated means to an end. It does, however, have effects, and I know it does, and that knowing is somehow part of my decision to give in to my anger.

Knowing anger's effects is vividly a part of my deciding to get angry by imaginatively reminding myself of, for instance, the angering boss's offenses. Such anger is voluntary. At the other extreme, volition is not a part of my explosion that happens before I know it. There is an intermediate case of giving in to anger, which is neither a clearly calculated decision, nor a purely spontaneous automaticity. Both the angering situation and knowing of the effects of anger are somehow relevant.

We are especially interested in the intermediate case because it is the closest to deciding to go berserk. Going berserk differs from mere anger in its intensity and, more importantly, in its duration and, most importantly of all, in its social meaning. The social meaning of anger is certainly relevant, and we are always sensitive to the fact that the longer the reaction, the greater its meaning. Also, we know that quick recoveries partly undo those meanings.

It is acceptable to get angry at many things, but even if I get angry when it is not expected, it is excusable to the extent it is short. Unexplained flashes of anger are not of great import as long as they are temporary and hurt no one. We can see that all this is different from going berserk. Going berserk may be spontaneous, but it cannot be as spontaneous as mere anger. It is a sustained state, a way of being that endures, and it is a well-known social role whose effects are, if not known in detail, widely understood in their general outline. Giving in to going berserk, then, is a commitment to a future in a way much more serious than getting angry. It is a commitment to a sustained state and to a social role. The "giving in" may also be passive, as when one gives in to anger. But sometimes, it is a passivity with a fuller proactive intentionality than merely getting angry.

Do we neglect the spontaneity of going berserk? I recall a prison inmate, out on work release, who was given strict instructions to return to the prison at 5:00 P.M. This was in Boston, and the subways were quite reliable and ran often at that time of day. All went well for nearly a week.

One afternoon, he discovered that he had no subway tokens, and no money to buy one. He panicked; he could only think of failing to meet the deadline. He dashed out of the subway station and began to run toward the prison, twelve miles away. Within a block he realized this was hopeless and became even more upset. He jumped into a car that was stopped for a light. It was driven by a woman, whom he ordered to take him to the prison. She became frightened and jumped out of the car and began screaming. He moved over to the driver's seat and took off, heading for the prison. Convinced the woman's screams had alerted the police, he ran several stoplights to avoid being caught. Eventually he sideswiped a bus and forced other cars to collide, and as he finally stacked the car up on a bridge abutment, he passed out, perhaps from exhaustion, perhaps from his head hitting the windshield.

We note in this case that the man's sense of the future was not absent. Indeed, it was fear of missing his deadline that motivated his extraordinary behavior. Had he behaved rationally, he would have pretended—but the particular future that permeated the present was not a commitment to a sustained state or a social role. This example appears to be a panic that led to increasingly hasty and self-defeating strategies, all in response to a larger situation in which the stakes were high. They eventuated in a rush of energy, mobilized in increasingly desperate attempts to meet the crisis.

The fact that there are examples of seemingly spontaneous episodes of going berserk does not imply that all episodes are like that. There are always background factors, and the frequent experience of going berserk, I think, is like giving in to anger—an intermediate case between spontaneous action and calculated action whose social meanings (effects on others, role definition, etc.) are known ahead of time.

The prison inmate on work release, like others who go berserk, interpreted his situation as one in which everything was at stake at once. Of course, the stakes were high, but his very being was not at stake. Being late in returning would have consequences, but his panic led him to put more at stake than there was in reality. Suppose I am alone at night reading a ghost story. I believe I hear the noise of a door open and shut—a door that I know is locked. I may say to myself, "Only something evil could have opened that door." At the same time, I know that reading a ghost story is suggestive and that I must be mistaken. I then feel a breeze swish past my face. A ghost? Surely not, but then what is it? The fireplace gives a startling crackle. Is it responding to the ghost? The evidence is beginning to pile up, but I keep one foot firmly in the world of ordinary life, for I know that believing such evidence is giving myself over to a world in which I am haunted, where my usual control is lost, and supernatural events may freely violate my mere naturalistic understanding.

If this ghost episode were the third consecutive evening of such events, and if I suddenly recall many similar patterns of then seemingly random accidents, then my suspicions would mount. I could conclude that I must, as a matter of simple self-protection, keep open the possibility that ghosts are haunting me. The possibility becomes a suspicion, and the suspicion becomes a conviction, in incremental steps, so that it is not clear just when I give into going berserk. But such a process is exactly one of our intermediate type—neither sudden nor spontaneous, nor calculated. Yet, being intermediate, it has aspects of both the other two. On the one hand, like spontaneous anger, there is something automatic about the course of events. I do not willingly choose to hear the door or feel the breeze. The inmate did not willing choose to be out of subway tokens. These events are forced on me and were forced on the inmate from outside ourselves. Was there an agency there? Someone who did it to me? On the other hand, while the automatisms of my emotions and perceptions may be beyond my control, they do not automatically carry my conviction that someone is out to get me. Of course, for the inmate, there is a sense in which that may be true, for prison authorities are not always kind.

In my case of the suspected ghost, the conviction is mine. I really must own it. A suspicion became a conviction only with my complicitous act. Convictions say, "Yes, by Jove, that's right!" and the conviction that "they are out to get me" becomes clear only after some indecision, some ambiguity that we willingly resolve. Such a willing may relieve tension between suspicions and common sense, and it may resolve a felt conflict and offer me a sense that I know what is going on. But it is exactly this conflict that offers other possibilities—possibilities that are closed off in the resolution of the conflict. Giving in to going berserk may be relieving or even satisfying, but it is not just a relief or a satisfaction. It is a relief or a satisfaction that closes off possibilities, narrows the future, and burns some bridges in polite society.

Anger and going berserk each offers us cases that are, in different ways, intermediate between automatisms and volitional planning. In the phenomena of pretending, they are also intermediate between ritualistic pretending, which is as inevitable as culture, and is both voluntary and necessary, on the one hand, and consciously purposeful pretending, on the other.

PURPOSEFUL PRETENDING

To pretend is to *pre*—(before hand, ahead of time)—*tend* (to stretch out), to plan ahead of time how one will act in the future. It is to forego normal spontaneity and act in a preplanned way. To the modern ear, it also means to feign, either in the spirit of play as in "let's pretend," or in the spirit of deceit, as in "you pretended you loved me." Both playful imitation for our amusement and deceitful falsification for our profit are familiar. Playful pretending ranges from a momentary mimic to the Shakespearean play. Deceitful pretending ranges from avoiding someone's eyes to the elaborate con game. But throughout these variations, we can see a common structure in pretending.

First of all, pretending establishes a second story line, however brief, alongside, or parallel, to my ordinary sense of who I am. In pretending, every act becomes double—a decision to pretend and an act I perform in pretending. The doubleness of the act is visible to the pretender, while the observer is supposed to see only the *pretended* act, not the *pretending* one. The doubleness is always there. Even though an actress throws herself so totally into her role that she forgets who she is, that forgetting is temporary and superficial. It is contextualized by the marginal presence of her real life. Pretending is inevitably duplicitous.

Second, pretending is a display for others. It is social, in origin at least. Whether it is an amusement or a scam, it, nevertheless, strives to convince the observer that the pretense is true to hide the doubleness of the story line and to keep one's real life from being visible. Of course, it is also not particularly rare that I pretend to myself. I tell myself I am charming when I know I am not, that I have a good poker hand when I should know better. Such self-deceptions will complicate the story later, but for now, we shall focus on the more social situation, where there is an actor and observer.

The tension between the two story lines is thus a tension between two persons, and actor and an observer. This tension can be selectively relieved, as when an actor breaks from his role and lets the audience see his real self. This is disappointing to an audience who wants to be deceived; it is funny to an audience who does not. In the case of deceitful pretending, any such break ruins the pretense. In the full scale con game, the pretender must bear all the tension him- or herself; he or she can neither share it nor get relief from it. His or her seriousness of purpose must be equal to the strains of the sustained pretense.

These two descriptive features of pretending are fairly simply stated, and they are fairly lucid at their face value. All of us understand doubling the story line of our lives by pretending, and we understand enacting the second line for the observer, while we, the actor, know another, first story line, which is our real lives.

We also see the difference between serious, deceitful pretending and playful pretending. We see that in playful pretending, we are not really keeping the secret; we are only pretending to do so. Playful pretending is another version of pretending to pretend. It is acting in a way designed to imitate an intention to deceive another without really doing so. Playful pretending toys with serious issues such as trust and deceit but with nothing really at stake. It is arguable that it is the structure of all play. It also, however, opens for us the entire realm of the imaginary, where the dynamics of fun, and all their variety, can be enacted. *Play* and *deceit* are two poles of pretending, in a finite field of possible interpersonal patterns.

We also playfully and deceitfully pretend for ourselves. Just as when the audience is others, pretending for myself is transparent in its pretense when it is playful and opaque when it is deceitful. I know when I am playfully kidding myself, and I enjoy it, but I do not know when I seriously deceive myself. When I playfully kid myself, it can be funny to others as well, and I may do it to amuse others. But when I seriously deceive myself, it is not likely to be funny. My self-deception presents others with a pretense that is, in at least one way, manipulative, for I need them to concur in my self-deception.

That kind of support from others is easily forthcoming in pretending to be depressed, to which we shall soon turn. If I seem sad, others may wish to take it seriously. I somehow am aware of this effect, and this can well come to bear on my giving in to depression. After all, a depressed person is a well-known character in our culture.

People feel sorry for those who have experienced a trauma. Pretending to be depressed is neither playful nor is it simply deceitful of others. It is a brand of pretending for oneself as well as for others. A more detailed analysis of pretending and depression is required, but first, we must inquire further into character and volition.

CHARACTER AND VOLITION

Armed with our ideas about the range of volition in the expression of feelings—from spontaneous sincerity (involuntary), through "giving in to" (partly involuntary), to duplicitous pretending (completely voluntary)—let us ask again about being who we are. I pointed out in chapter 1 our culture's cast of characters and how our second consciousness monitors our being who we are with an eye toward the question "Am I enacting the self I want to enact?" This question is at once a question about my appearance to others—whether I am making the right impression—and a question about my fulfilling myself—according to an ideal self I strive to be. In both cases, the culture's stock of characters supplies me with categories of being and with agreed-upon criteria of these categories.

To what extent is my being who I am a matter of spontaneous sincerity? To what extent is it duplicitous pretending—or that intermediate case of giving in to a pattern that is partly spontaneous but also seems somehow to require my assent? The answers to these questions change as we move in our being from character to character and from one to another situation, or time in life. Adolescents in an identity crisis explicitly try out various selves. Newlyweds try to be the husband or wife they think their spouse wants them to be. When I begin a new job, I consciously try to behave to fit my employer's expectations, and when I have children, I intentionally behave in imitation of the "good parent"—as I understand that character.

These intentional pretendings are not quite deceptive, for we want to be who we want to be, not just to pretend. But they are not quite sincere either, in that their successes are reckoned on the basis of feedback

I get, rather than on the basis of my own decisions. Of course, I may desire only to fulfill the character and to get confirming feedback, but such a desire is inherently duplicitous, since it adds a second agenda to my spontaneous interests: an image to project for others. As long as this addition involves no conflict, the duplicity may not matter at all to me. I may further minimize the tension of the pretending by redefining the character in such a way that I need not try very hard. That kind of independence, however, runs the risk—and I know it—of disappointing important people around me, whose expectations matter to me.

All this pretending does not preclude the possibility that despite my best effort, let's say, to be a good husband, as I understand that character, I enact instead a clumsy oaf. If I am trying to be the good husband and actually produce a close replica of the clumsy oaf, the reason may be that my own enculturation, which taught me the cast of characters, was incomplete or biased by the peculiarities of my history. We might think of this as a cultural difference.

However, if there is no cultural difference, and my cast of characters is adequately similar to that of my wife and our friends, then the discrepancy between my intended enactment and my actual production is more complex. The clumsy oaf is apparently sincere; he emerges as a self I am in spite of my efforts to pretend otherwise. Indeed, part of my clumsiness may be exactly my inability to pretend successfully, which is another way of saying that my skill at duplicity is lacking—that my ability to live convincingly up to cultural ideals is deficient. The struggle to live up to cultural ideals—the good husband, the good parent, the good doctor—is well known and is, by definition, calculative and anything but spontaneous. It is admirable, perhaps, but no less duplicitous for that.

Less admirable is sincerity from people whose motives include the temptation to embarrass me. I want them rather to pretend they are decent and to work hard enough at that pretense so that I am convinced. I want the act to be convincing, and I want them to invest in it as much as I do. That is perhaps not too different from how the more decent among us got to be decent in the first place.

The struggle for goodness, however, is also subject to failure. Indeed, the term "goodness," without which human beings would not be civilized, denotes a perfection that is not really available, on a long-term basis, to human beings. If I say that Fred is a good man, I must be understood to be saying that he is relatively good, compared to other men. I am not saying he fulfills the criteria of goodness absolutely. Human beings never do, and we also, as human beings, always know it.

In addition to the struggle for perfection, and existing side-by-side with it making it meaningful, are two other human temptations: (1) giving in to something less than the really good self, and (2) behaving spontaneously and sincerely regardless of where that behavior falls on the scale of goodness. The latter alternative, of spontaneous sincerity, is, curiously, recommended in some quarters of our culture and was stylish in the 1960s counterculture: "If it feels good, do it." Of course, a realization that what feels best for me hurts others often leads me not to do so. But as before, the intermediate case, the former alternative of giving in to something less than the good self, is at once more common, more problematic, and more interesting. Here, we are not speaking of ideal characters whose goodness is nonconflictual (I have rarely found myself giving in to goodness). We are speaking rather about that vast array of less-than-perfect characters that make up all of us. Because of our imperfections, we are able to accept and understand the behavior of others and of ourselves.

Note the cultural relativity in this. The hermaphrodite, a person born with sex organs of both sexes, is highly revered among the Navaho Indians. In our culture, we do not allow such a person to exist. There is no such character in our stock of characters, and persons born hermaphroditic are, at a young age, surgically "corrected" to be either one sex or the other.[1] Similarly, subcultures vary. A college community contains the character "nerd," while middle school students in my home town speak of "speds" (special education students), and so on. These are variations within the larger culture, where the names change, but the concept, the actual character, may or may not.

Among one of the most striking things about the recent 20th century may have been, in the West at least, the assimilation by the culture of psychiatric categories into its common stock of characters. Of course, such an assimilation could not occur before there was a well-established psychiatry—a 20th-century phenomenon. But the pervasiveness of these categories enables us to do such striking things as to understand Nazism as an illness and the annihilation of six million European Jews as an example of psychopathology.

Since when is genocide a disease? Do we not more unequivocally call it evil? On the other hand, our peculiar modern naturalization of evil can be seen in our unusual ability to make things formerly called "evil" comprehensible to ourselves as illness. Sometimes this thought erases a moral presence and leads us to blame a force in the universe or an aspect of human nature. This traditional struggle with evil is a more desperate struggle than ever before, since our killing capability has become progressively more cataclysmic. Sometimes our naturalization of evil is a denial that there is a moral struggle, and it pretends there is a medical one.

This confusion is also a later version of our historical and contemporary ambivalence toward madness, sometimes yielding sympathy, sometimes ridicule and contempt. At the very least we must note additions to our culture's cast of characters: the paranoid, the anorexic, the depressed, and so on—all new refinements of the earlier madman or lunatic. Each diagnostic distinction makes the strange familiar and shores up an implicit confidence in modernity—a confidence that we now understand these people, for they are, after all, only suffering from an illness. Illness, unlike evil, is no mystery.

However, the relationship between psychiatric types and evil remains. It is related in a complicated way to how we experience our selves, or judge in others, giving in to being neurotic, phobic, or depressed. That is, giving in to such a character-to-be is at once an admission of one's failure and an excuse for it. But at a deeper level, it is also at once an admission of one's evil and at the same time a delivery from culpability for that evil. Psychiatry, as we say, has replaced religion—that arena of life formerly responsible for a recognition of our shortcomings and for our forgiveness and redemption in spite of them.

Before the cash value of these interpretations can be reckoned, we shall have to examine the psychology of being abnormal much more closely. Depression is our main example.

SUMMARY

Human behavior is inherently duplicitous, in contrast to the world-absorbed, pre-reflective consciousness of a blue jay. My second consciousness is preoccupied with judgments of myself, myself as seen through the eyes of others. I know, and know that others know, just what kinds of judgments are being made, and I inevitably gauge my behavior to those judgments. This gauging is a second motive—secondary to my other, sincere motive, but no less present and no less important.

By calling such psychological processes "duplicitous," we are describing the resulting psychological doubleness. But we are also focusing on that place where psychologically driven behavior overlaps with morally judged behavior—an overlap that engages both historical and contemporary tendencies to moralize illness, as well as to medicalize evil.

One gauge of duplicity is its spontaneity: the more spontaneous a behavior is, the less it is calculated and geared to its effects on others, and the more sincere it is. Anger is often (but not always) sincere. Outright pretending is exactly not spontaneous and hence is fully duplicitous. The intermediate case, giving in to some cultural script that we know and others will understand, is really a range of possible mixtures of spontaneous sincerity and pretentious duplicity.

We give in to being the characters we are, selected from aspects of our existing reputation and from the cultural stock of characters. Along with struggling to fulfill ideals, these enactments are duplicitous, which is to say only that they engage us in complex motives and compromise our single-minded sincerity. The culture's evolving stock of characters has come to include psychiatric types. This development is a modern attempt to comprehend what we do not understand—to demystify particularly what used to be called evil. There is a way, then, that giving into being a psychiatric type is an individual version of our culture's larger struggle with mystery, and especially with evil.[2]

Much psychopathology is in this intermediate range, neither involuntary sincerity nor voluntary pretending and must, therefore, be understood in that way. The most serious pathology, we shall see, has lost its duplicity and its pretentiousness; it is utterly sincere. Much depression is, fortunately, duplicitous. Some depression, unfortunately, is not.

CHAPTER THREE

~

Pretending and Depression

DEPRESSION

It is helpful to define "depression" first in its more extreme, pure, and accomplished form. This strategy enables us to anchor our observations of the various states we clinically call depression, to clarify an essence, a presence, a possibility in all our lives.

Depression is not a symptom. Symptoms are signs of struggle, of an attempt to preserve, enhance, or defend a center, such as myself, as an ongoing enterprise that is moving out of the past into a future. That future may be terrifying, and I may be avoiding the terror; or the past may be humiliating, and I may be escaping the humiliation, but there is movement nonetheless. Symptoms struggle with the movement, the passage of time, and in doing so *I am*, my *being is*, temporally and vitally.

Depression is different from all this. It is the opposite of a symptom. In depression, my moving into the future has stopped; the passage of time promises nothing but a dreary repetition of the past—no growth, no openness, no future, as we ordinarily understand it. It is hard to say that *I am*, in depression, for my being has ceased that essential human activity of moving into the future. Further, there is nothing to defend when I am depressed. If there were, I would still be struggling, but I have given up the struggle and now just persist in it, out of inertia, a kind of mechanical extension of myself into the future but with no anticipation, no hope. Without a future to negotiate and a self to defend, I have lost my vitality, my life. I am paradoxically without movement in a context of flux, dead but still alive, suffering life without life's purpose, death without death's sleep.[1]

As with symptoms, depression runs counter to rationality and violates the rules of reality. It also runs counter to and violates the enthusiasm of life, that vital force that lies so deep in our being that we fail to notice it until it is absent, as in death, or blocked and negated, as in depression. Over one hundred years ago, Søren Kierkegaard (1941) said:

Despair is never ultimately over the external object but always over ourselves. A girl loses her sweetheart and despairs. It is not over the sweetheart, but over herself-without-the-sweetheart.

Kierkegaard continues:

And so it is with all cases of loss, whether it be money, power, or social rank. The unbearable loss is not really in itself unbearable. What we cannot bear is being stripped of the external object. We stand denuded and see the intolerable abyss of ourselves.[2]

"Oneself" was an abyss to Kierkegaard because of man's alienation from God, his source and his destiny. Sigmund Freud, three-quarters of a century later, also spoke of loss, its role in depression and the struggles with the self that follow. Oneself becomes an intolerable abyss for Freud when mourning fails, when, in the absence of the lost object, our love and our hatred turn back on ourselves in a convoluted orgy of guilt— oneself becoming intolerable and abysmal.

Modern psychologists don't necessarily construe the universe as either Kierkegaard or Freud did, but we, nevertheless, are indebted to their insights. In depression, it is oneself that is the issue, as Kierkegaard said, and mourning a loss is a crucial part of emerging from depression, as Freud suggested. We might put it this way: The work of mourning is the work of becoming someone new after a loss, of creating a new way of being oneself, now in the absence of an anchor in the world that formerly tied one down to a definition of oneself in society, space, and time (Keen, 1984).

Those things we lose, about which we get depressed—a lover, for example— define us when they are here and leave us undefined when they abandon us. We rebel against the loss, but more importantly, we rebel against being someone else, against being some other way. Emerging from depression, then, is essentially a matter of reinventing ourselves (Keen, 1984).

Now, we will explore depression in its various forms, in light of pretending and duplicity as well as spontaneity and sincerity. We want to look more closely at how culture frames our behavior with agreements and fills our self-consciousness with themes and characters and judgments. We also want to examine the varieties of what we have been calling "the intermediate case"—that area between purposeful pretending and spontaneous sincerity—and how these varieties appear in depression.

CLINGING TO THE PAST AND CONSTRICTING THE FUTURE

A divorce, a death in the family, the loss of one's job are the types of insults from the world that create crisis. They chip away at, and crucially undermine, one's sense of self, one's certainty about who one is and what one thinks. In the face of such crises, one loses track of what one wants, fears, and hopes for.

The insults invade the order of the past, rearranging relevancies, so that I lose track of which memories matter and in what way. As I lose touch with where I am coming from, I also find that my direction—where I'm going, and certainly where I currently stand—are all thrown into doubt. What was solid becomes shaky. As I look for something to orient myself—a relationship, an activity, perhaps just a thought—I find solidness where I didn't expect it, but in a shape I cannot fathom. What I understand has lost its solidity and what is solid is no longer understood.

In such a crisis, I pretend—I play at; I imitate; I put myself on, and others, as if I know who I am. This pretending seems to be my only alternative to giving in to the chaos of my doubt and my uncertainty. Remembered fragments of who I have been guide me into what to pretend. "They know me as serious, so I'll be serious." But these fragments are unreliable. I fabricate the whole out of the part, and I move ahead into the future feigning the certainty of an ordinary person. But the whole is shaped wrongly. The part from which it was created occupies too great a portion, and I behave stupidly.

The pretended nature of who I am becomes apparent to me, and I fear it shows. Others who see me are a threat, but the danger is much more than embarrassment, or even shame. The collapse of the pretense does more than blow my cover. It reveals a core I am trying to hide from myself. It throws me face to face with my own emptiness, uncertainty, and panic.

Like other pretending, this pretending throws me into a doubleness and a deception. The self I extend out for others to see runs side by side with a self I am hiding, a self who is manipulating the showing, calculating what will show and hiding the terrible fact that I do not really know what I think, what I want, who I am. I seize upon feedback I get in order to shore up the act. I build the presentation out of remembered fragments and perceived approvals, and the whole I put together begins to coalesce. I even forget that it is a pretense. I pretend I'm not pretending, and I begin to live the pretense as if it were myself. The self I am hiding becomes hidden from myself. My hiding pretends to be living and my living becomes a hidden hiding.

The losses, in divorce or death or unemployment, are well known to everyone. We even have more or less codified social roles of divorcé, bereaved, and unemployed. These roles aid immeasurably in our pretending. They tell us how to pretend, and they tell us what to pretend. They engage us in reciprocities with others playing reciprocal roles—sympathizers mostly, but also exploiters to beware of and people-who-don't-know, to pretend for—a whole social fabric to weave ourselves into.

Helpful as this social fabric and these roles are in the short run, they tempt us into falsifications that make pretending into something much more dangerous than its usual appearance as play or simple deception. When pretending is part of our coping with crisis, it joins with clung-to social roles to create an entire life-world of seeming sense but secret sham. In addition, the help offered by the social roles is temporary; I am not expected to continue my mourning indefinitely. In its wisdom, the culture accepts my pretending while the crisis is "critical," but it later rejects attempts to make a career of this role. The entire pretend life-world, which accepts the certainty of the social role in the face of the uncertainty of crisis, is a loan, obtained by taking a lien on my soul. To retain the loan is to forfeit the lien and finally to forfeit my soul.

The crisis pretense is hardly pathological. To grasp at fragments, to fear the uncertainty and try to cover it up, to accept the social role and its mask—the social loan—are merciful alternatives to terror. They are existentially rational. However, when I extend the crisis pretense beyond its time, I am engaging a chronic pretense. In this sense, chronic pretending originates in crisis, or in the language of more traditional theory, psychopathology originates in trauma.

When I engage in this pretending, either temporarily or chronically, I am formulating a future into which to thrust myself as I have always felt myself going someplace. But the future I construct is built upon fragments of the past—a past me who is no longer me. My future is thus being shaped in my forcing my memory on it. This forced future is false; it clings to the past and constricts possibilities, but it seems preferable to the threatening and unpredictable future of a self, now without its anchor—a future self I do not know and have not met, and whose existential possibilities I refuse to explore.

DENYING THE PAST AND EXTRAVAGATING THE FUTURE

As previously described, life's insults provoke me to cling to the past and thus to constrict the future with limits borrowed from the past I no longer am. But I also do something else. I deny the loss, and by denying the loss, I deny those claims the past *does have* on my future, and I therefore falsify my future in the direction of extravagance.

Suppose that my father dies. I am his son; that is who I am. In his absence, that *who* loses some of its reality. I still am his son, but no longer does his fatherly gaze reassure me as to who I am. I must, with his death, fill up a gap in myself. I must become someone else—not someone entirely new, of course, but someone whose anchors of identity fasten my stability somewhere else through the shifting winds of life.

Now, of course, I know he is gone. Consciously, the cognition is there. "I know" he is dead and "I know" that I know it. There is no ambiguity. But at the fringe of my consciousness, I still take note of things to tell him, or I think I see him in the street, or I find myself listening for the phone at the accustomed time of his call. These fringe phenomena do not mean that I am denying his death, for "I know" he is dead. But the world I live in still bears his presence. This world does not know he is gone. I know he is not there, but the life-world I have created and inhabit still has him alive. How could this be? The fact that "I know" he is dead makes it needless to confront that world. But as long as that world is intact, every waking realization of what "I know" angers me. But since "I accept" my father's death, the anger too seems unlike me and remains beyond the edge of my consciousness. Why should I be angry? "I know he is gone. I'm not denying it. I'm an adult. I accept it." In other words, I deny my anger.

But at the edge of my consciousness, I lose patience with the car that won't start, the student who misunderstands, with the weather. Small irritations seem to magnify themselves. The world now appears to me to be a succession of inconveniences, a series of ordinary things that become contemptible. I locate the origin of this contempt in the things in the world. The visible world becomes discolored and dreary. The livable world becomes less livable, but I still do not feel my anger, for I convince myself that my impatience with the world has nothing to do with a denial because, after all, "I know" my father has died. Things cannot continue this way. The discoloration of the world threatens to reveal to me my anger, and my anger threatens to reveal to me the falsity of my "acceptance" of my loss, and the falsity of that acceptance threatens to confront me with the necessity to reinvent myself.

Without denying for a minute what I know to be true, I re-create the world—not into a world truly without my father—but rather into a world where the inconveniences do not matter, where discolorations are unimportant, where nothing irritates me. Ordinary things, so recently contemptible, now become quite acceptable or even fascinating. The tempo of the world speeds up, and I find that knowing my father has died seems not to matter very much at all.

This struggle, between what I know as an isolated fact, but cannot face as a restructured world, leads me to reinvent the world so I do not have to face reinventing myself. It yields a denial as important, though not as obvious, as if I were simply to insist that my father lives on. It also is not as obvious as keeping a dead child's room just as it was when the child was alive, or refusing to get rid of the dog house or bird cage after their inhabitants have died—material world remnants of a past now gone.

Indeed, this denial is more subtle and more global, more invisible and more important. Both are pretenses, but the doghouse pretense does not also pretend not to be a pretense. It is pretending temporarily; its inconsistency with what I know makes its resolution only a matter of time. Misconstruing the world, in contrast, has no such obvious absurdity. It shores up a series of denials, by the way discoloring the world, hiding my anger, displaying my pretense at knowing. If I can keep the world the same, even knowing that "he is gone" I undermine the necessity of reinventing myself. In shoring up these denials, this preservation of the world pretends seriously; it pretends not to be a pretense.

When I pretend seriously, in this way, I admit my sense of loss, but my experiential world does not change; I lose my openness to many things in the world and in myself, and I move into a future peculiarly unrestrained by certain features of the past. To cut the future loose from the past, to sever the ties between origin and destiny, of who I have been and who I will be, is to open up a world of extravagance. Ordinary things may become fascinating.

Misconstruing the world to be as it was before my loss may not seem very extravagant, but to construct the world as the same (a denial), while asserting that, in fact, he is dead (denying a denial), cuts me free from dealing with the loss of anchors in the past. Experiencing the *absence* of these anchors, without dealing with the *loss* of these anchors, opens up the future of possibilities untempered by the ties to past necessities, an openness whose structure owes no debts, has no obligations, is free to be ecstatic, or peaceful, or whatever I want.

Pretending has now lost its obligation to deceive others, for the audience is no longer others, it is, rather, myself. Such pretending is both harder and easier to carry out. It is harder because "I know" I am doing it, but like knowing my father died, such knowledge can be isolated from the world and made inconsequential. The pretending is easier because I no longer must reinvent the world. Others have recast the world without my father, even if they do not focus on losing him. I know I have lost him but continue to live in an unchanged world. They live in a changed world, while I do not. Since I know he is dead, I pretend only for myself, not for others.

PRETENDING AND PSEUDODEPRESSION

Extravagating the future is the opposite of constricting the future. In *constricting* the future, I cling to a fragment of the past and limit the future to its contours so as to avoid having to change. In *extravagating* the future, I deny a part of the past and thus disconnect the future from those enduring structures that limit the future to a certain identity and obligation to origins. I do this to avoid staying the same. I avoid changing because the challenge of reinventing myself is terrifying. I avoid staying the same because that sameness includes a loss that is terrifying. These are opposite movements; both enacted to avoid the terrors of life, and at their center, the activity of pretending joins them together into a single posture or style.

Much depression, therefore (ought we to say much of life?), is pretending. However, these pretenses *in* depression do not yet describe pretending to be depressed. Are these phenomena pretending *in* depression, where the clinical entity, depression, is "the phenomenon" and pretending can be shown to be part of it? Or are these phenomena depression *in* pretense, where "the phenomenon" is pretending and depression can be shown to be part of it?

Are we analyzing depression by seeing pretending, or are we able to say, after doing so, that pretending is what we see, the main phenomenon, and depression is some part of *that*? Perhaps we are like my grandmother who darned my blue socks with green yarn. With each succeeding darning, the blue socks with green patches became green socks with blue patches, until finally we saw that the socks were not blue at all but were green. Unlike my grandmother, however, we can say, "They were green all the time; I just misunderstood." We have been looking at pretending all the time; we just misunderstood by calling it depression. Most clinical presentations of depression are pretense. Real depression, that paradoxical giving up of life in the midst of it, is really quite rare.

Our conclusion must be, when we look at pretending in depression, that the tail wags the dog. When we look at pretending in depression, we find that pretending is the main activity, and if there is depression here at all, it is secondary to pretending. Indeed, pretending to be depressed is not being depressed at all. There can be little doubt that pretending to be depressed makes us anxious. Such activity is accompanied by the marginal (occasionally even focal) awareness that the secret could be revealed. Pretending has the same kind of sense of instability, like the impending collapse of a house of cards, that characterizes lying in general.

This sense of collapse is a sense of an impending disclosure that will reveal my sham, embarrass me before others, and confront me with what I am hiding from myself. This sense of ever-near disaster is much closer to what we call anxiety than it is to depression. Keeping a secret does not happen in real depression, for in depression, I have given up. There is no reason to keep a secret; I am sustaining no illusions, for myself or others. Anxiety about impending disclosure of my duplicity is to engage a struggle, whereas depression is exactly the giving up of the struggle.

Pretending to be depressed is an anxious activity that keeps secrets from others and sustains illusions for myself. It is my attempt to avoid the task of redefining myself, and so it constricts the future by clinging to the past. It is also my attempt to avoid staying the same insofar as the same self I am is the self who has sustained a loss too frightening to face. I, therefore, extravagate the future by denying that aspect of my past that confronts me with loss.

Finally, pretending to be depressed is a way of struggling with all this by imitating themes: the depressive themes of guilt and helplessness and hopelessness. But this imitation is not exactly hopeless. It is hopeful that the imitation will magically yield some of the joy of life that one has sensed losing.

Pretending to be depressed is anxiety. It is not depression at all. Pretending to be depressed is a way of being in the world in the face of crises and losses, a way that tries to cope with a future, however inauthentically or self-deceptively. Depression in its pure form gives up trying to cope. Pretending to be depressed is, therefore, pseudodepression.

DUPLICITY AND HEALTH

Pretending to be depressed—pseudodepression—is duplicitous; real depression, real giving up, real ceasing to struggle, is sincere. This sincere state strikes us as much more puzzling, even paradoxical, and certainly as more pathological, than the duplicities of pretending to be depressed. The duplicities continue life's struggle; they are therefore more like our health than our illness, more like life than death. The duplicities of pseudodepression are often preoccupied with the issues of becoming someone new and remaining the person I've always been. Changing and staying the same are human—not subhuman—problems. They are problems of remembering, of self-consciousness.

Remembering and self-consciousness also partake of characters and themes provided by the culture, and at least during the short run, we cannot call them pathological at all. Losses frighten us, so we need to borrow the role of loser in order to survive anxiety. Losses also sadden us, so we need such roles to survive the sadness.

Finally, however, the anxiety of being a new self is the challenge, the uncertainty of continuing my official identity—my name, rank, and serial number—without knowing exactly who that now is. I eventually must face an uncertain future, and that makes me anxious, and I must face a certain past, including a loss, and that makes me sad. Can I be a self, a me, again? Pretending postpones this challenge by protecting me from both the sadness of the past and the anxiety of the future. For a while, that pretending is prescribed and approved of by the culture, and its reciprocal roles are enacted by other members of the culture.

After a while, it is assumed that there is no further need for pretense. If it continues, it will become idiosyncratic, no longer a part of a ritual understood by others. It loses touch with the hierarchy of agreements that frame my interaction with others. "I'm so depressed I could slit my wrists." What is at stake here? Ambiguity appears. The cultural hierarchy of agreements is in question. On the other hand, I reinvent the world in some extravagant way, desperately concealing my desperation and concealment but vulnerable to being exposed. Just as the suicide threat *may be* histrionic, so the cheerful recovery *may be* a house of cards. The stakes of everything become ambiguous. Culture has ceased to supply me and my interlocutors with a framework wherein we know what our actions mean to one another.

My second consciousness, the one that imagines your view of me as a way to be understandable to you, becomes confused and your second consciousness does too. Is my suicide threat only to impress you (duplicitous)? Or is it sincere? Is my good cheer so brittle that it could collapse any time? You begin to have real difficulty dealing with me. Meanwhile, I can see, with my second consciousness, your difficulty. Your difficulty is my difficulty. I'm obviously not making the impression I want to make. I am duplicitous when I want to be sincere and sincere when I want to be duplicitous. Do I mean the suicide threat? Is my good cheer brittle? Your confusion about these issues doubles my already existing confusion about them.

Throughout all this confusion, much of which is created by pretending and pretending to pretend, we must remember that the pretending and the duplicity are the healthy, the struggling, the vital parts of the picture. The same suicide threat uttered simply, sincerely, and unequivocally is much more ominous. It is better to be tangled in these pretenses and duplicities than to give up. But it is better for the pretenses and duplicities to be intelligible to others than it is for them to be confused and create confusion. The challenge we see is to move not from pretense to sincerity but to move from tangled pretense to a cultural one, from ambiguity to intelligibility.

Nothing could be more foolish at this point in our confusion than to call for sincerity, for single-meaninged utterances that symbolize nothing else. This would denude us of culture's complexity and reduce us to a single-mindedness, and the single-mindedness of loss and its confusions open the possibility of true giving up. Consider a funeral. I am sad and frightened after the death of someone close. My perplexity may be paralyzing. At the same time, I know what I have to do. I have to be a survivor, a mourner who lets everyone know that I am not destroyed by the loss. I am expected to mourn in public, to express my sadness by engaging in a public role of mourning survivor.

This demand, placed on me by my culture, can be obviated only in special circumstances. It is not an obligation I want to have. I must be brave when I feel sad, frightened, perhaps even paralyzed. I am obligated to make a showing, to don the mask of courage, primarily for the benefit of the community, the public—friends and relatives but not people who really know how I feel, or to whom I can show my feelings, at least not completely. The unadulterated completeness of mourning terrifies even me.

The rituals are fairly standard. Prayers, a eulogy, perhaps a viewing, and always that final lowering of the casket into the ground—conclusively, the marking of the grave as a site of remembrance. As I traverse these rituals, I am wearing a mask. I am duplicitous, enacting courage I don't feel, expressing sadness, mourning aloud even, but in role, as part of a public ritual. But when we realize what is accomplished in this ritual, this culturally prescribed duplicity, it can only be seen as healthy. Having traversed the rituals, I have demonstrated courage I did not know I had. The others who came were sad too, and while they couldn't know how I felt, I could see we shared the loss. I and they together traversed a transition; the community is there, mine, and I am theirs. I am not alone. Finally, and most important, the ritual accomplished the burial with the all-important marking of the gravesite. That gravesite makes a place for the lost beloved in the lives of the living. I may visit, or not; I know it is always there, an unimpeachable public and objective representation of my personal memories. Every time I visit the gravesite I relive the funeral; I join my personal loss to the loss of others; I mix my memories with theirs; I enact our continuing to live together.

Such is the shape of culturally prescribed mourning, which insists I don a mask and enact a ritual, even against my own sense of what I may want to do, or even what I believe I *can* do. That mask both hides and reveals; eventually its hiding and revealing are the same as I move from a solitary mourner to a communal one. The duplicity—particularly the consciousness of myself in the eyes of others, and how that compromises my sincerity—is guided by the culture into an achievement of mourning, of burial, of sharing, of remembering—and of continuing, like others, to live. This is a better pretense, a healthier duplicity, than pretending to be depressed. The main difference is the intelligibility of the mask, the public and ritual character of the pretending, which does not engage me in anxiously hiding from others but in exactly disclosing, revealing not only my sadness but also my courage and my solidarity with others. Yet there is nothing so simple as sincerity here. The layers of duplicity are manifold. What makes the ritual and discourse healthy is that they embody culture and hence are intelligible to the community, which in turn protects me from my greatest fear, my loneliness, and, finally, from my giving up—the possibility of pure depression.

A cultural ritual engages me in duplicities that are intelligible. Pretending to be depressed enacts a character, also borrowed from the cultural stock, and also lending myself a certain intelligibility. But pretending to be clinically depressed is also a certain acceptance of failure, and at another level, of evil, even as it is a ritualized attempt to deal with both. Pretending to be depressed fails, whereas mourning succeeds. Pretending also calls up the mysteries it attempts to cover up, but it falsely claims that, through psychology, unintelligible aspects of life become intelligible. The loss is exactly not intelligible.

At the same time, pretending to be depressed enacts another, more destructive kind of mystery. In so doing, it suggests mental illness, which finally undermines the cultural agreements upon which we all depend. The ambiguity of a suicide threat, for example, reinstates the mystery one is trying to cope with by calling oneself "depressed." It enacts the unintelligibility born of human complexity, even as it tries, and because of its means of trying, to make it intelligible.

Funerals, we see, do much better. At the center of these dynamics is the issue of human meaning and intelligibility. Our exploration of that issue in the next chapter will enable us to penetrate the meaning not only of pseudodepression but of real depression as well.

CHAPTER FOUR

Depression and Meaning

NARRATIVE AND MEANING

I began thinking of people in terms of their narratives because patient after patient told me a story—*their* story. The story was not always clear, and sometimes I had to urge them to tell it, but invariably people have a story to tell and that story is who they are.

Narratives have all the structures of human experience: central actors and events within a setting, with a past that is remembered and a future that is anticipated, in a context of relationships of love and hate, and a culture of good and evil.[1]

It has probably been only in the last several centuries that the narratives people live are so singularly personal, that is, centered around the person of oneself, with the time span bounded by birth and death, the characters limited to self and auxiliaries, and the space one's residences and haunts. Certainly before the 16th century, the story lived by most people in the West was the story told in sacred texts, and it was about individuals as only minor actors in a drama of God in the cosmos, interacting with people but not most centrally with people as individuals.

The time boundaries, space markers, indeed the world design, were different. As we look back at Christian Rome, we see an integration of local and cosmic stories, and the same is true with the ancient Hebrews and Egyptians. The first-century Christians and the fourth-century

BC. Athenians are especially interesting, for they show us stories in the process of radical and yet lasting change. The human self appears somewhat differently in each period, but never so vividly as in modern times. In the 18th-, 19th-, and especially 20th centuries, cosmos is reduced to mere backdrop, and even local units such as nations and families eventually give way to the self as the central focus of the narratives we live.

I recall a conference on autobiographies, where one of the participants was a publisher, who said that there had been periods in his memory when it seemed everyone had an autobiography to publish. Movie stars and sports figures, cab drivers and prostitutes, old people, and the most recent addition: young people. He was especially skeptical of the value of this last group and reported one agent who was trying to sell him the autobiography of an eleven-year-old. He was not reassured by the agent's guarantee that the author had the wisdom of someone twice his age.

Everyone's story is, of course, bound to his or her own perspective. You cannot help but notice, for example, in my account of a fight with my boss, that you are hearing only one side of the story. Furthermore, I am often unaware of the limits of my own perspective, of how my particular slant on things is just that—a particular slant—instead of an objective truth. As you listen to my story about my boss, you may be impressed with how my particular slant on things throws into bold relief whatever would justify me and obscure whatever might implicate me. At other times, you notice how my perspective seems to exaggerate my own weakness, fault, and culpability. This is also—and I shall return to this point—a kind of justification, a self-explaining, if not self-serving, kind of exercise.

Beyond that, one's story—and by now I am no longer limiting myself to patients but am describing my friends and myself too—guides one into the future as well. It ties the future options to past determinants by the coherence inherent in the narratives. That is, a narrative demands a certain order and interrelatedness of parts in order to be recognized as a story one can follow. Bartenders don't become stockbrokers, and vice versa. These stays of coherence are usually arranged so as to make one future option appear to be the right one, given who we've been, and other options to be wrong, incoherent, or—according to rules never quite articulatable—somehow dissonant.

The most important feature of my narrative, however, is beyond even this. It is the fact that my narrative makes myself intelligible to myself and to others. My story is my intelligibility. Insofar as I am not a nervous stutterer in the babble of life, grating abrasively against my past, my future, and my present situations, it is because I understand who I am—or perhaps I should say, because I have an understanding of who I am—which protects me from the chaos and anxiety of being no one intelligible. That understanding wards off having no place, no identity, no roles, functions, nor ways of mattering in the context of everyday experience. It is practically impossible to imagine my life without my story. Indeed, my life could no longer be mine, for my self is that story. There is no me, or mine, without it.

Returning now to my patients, I have listened, as we all have, to many stories, and we find that they may be characterized from the outside as biased and self-serving, but they have to be characterized from the inside as the framework within which everyday experience becomes intelligible.

Patients differ from other people in that they are also telling us about something that is not intelligible. There is a catch somewhere—a symptom that seems to them alien, or a relationship that keeps getting out of control, or a mood they cannot explain, or at the very least a person who tells them that something is drastically wrong—even if they themselves do not sense it. Almost always, of course, they do; they sense something is radically out of joint in the narrative they tell, enact, and are. In one sense, this out-of-joint something is part of, even the center of, the story they have to tell. That which was unintelligible to them, in the 20th century, became intelligible as one of those psychological misfortunes that befalls people, as a symptom, by definition unintelligible but, because it fulfills that qualification of a symptom or a psychological disturbance of some kind, it becomes intelligible.

This intelligibility of what was unintelligible is the by-product of their telling their story to a psychologist. Such an act not only "adopts the patient role," as we say, it changes a former narrative of someone who didn't have a psychological problem to a new narrative of someone who for a long time did not, and then did—or someone who has always had one, and so on.

Because we are all human, pretense and duplicity enter the picture. My intelligibility comes from my second layer, my reflective level of consciousness, which sometimes tells me that I have an emotional illness. Not everyone believes that emotional illnesses can befall him or her, but most of us believe it is possible.

Psychology interacts with ordinary life. It even affects the requirements for coherence in a narrative, by loosening them, by making exceptions plausible, by allowing essentially incoherent elements to become a part of a coherent story without changing most of the intelligibility of the story as a whole. Psychology, with its diagnostic categories, gives us explanations; it tells us how to make a kind of sense out of what in ourselves is unintelligible. There have always been such loosening influences. Erik Erikson (1958) reports that Martin Luther had no difficulty assuming that unexpected noises, or even his own fainting, was the work of the Devil, the personage of evil and chaos.

Similarly, Odysseus blamed Poseidon for his troubles, Orestes claimed Apollo told him to kill his mother, some people blame voodoo, and so on. Psychology today plays the role that was played by supernatural personages in the past, giving the unintelligible a kind of intelligibility that enables the coherence of my narrative to stay more or less intact in the face of things about myself that don't make sense. The difficulty with all these ways of including the unintelligible without damaging the intelligibility of the whole narrative is that they are enormously conservative. If my life demands a new understanding, which changes who I think I am, where I came from, or where I am going, then the understanding offered by popular psychology, a psychology of symptoms, like earlier superstitions, works against that change. It is a lot easier to modify my narrative by adding a psychological difficulty than it is to reinterpret my past, present, and future, to become someone different from the hero of my former narrative.

In fact, most patients want both—to stay the same, including their psychological misfortune, and to grow from whatever and whoever they have been, which has produced this mess, to someone else who can negotiate life without it. At the very least, patients want relief from symptoms, and if that relief is available through a quick fix such as psychopharmacology, then a desire to grow, or to change how or who they are may well be blunted.

What we ought to want for patients is not just an elimination of symptoms. Indeed, we have the sense that symptoms are not randomly added to a life; they are an integral part of how one handles one's situation as a whole. The story enacted has somehow produced symptoms; eliminating symptoms may or may not involve changing that story. It may or may not require change in the character I've been playing, that my understanding of my past and future change and that I enact a slightly (or grossly) different character, with a different past and future, in a different setting, engaging different people.

The desired goal of therapy rarely involves that I step out of my life and family and begin again as someone else—although that is sometimes a lovely fantasy. The particulars of the character, the setting, and so on, are all particulars in how I construe my character, the setting of my life. The elements of a narrative are internally related; to change any of them actually is to change them all. To change these things then is to change the narrative I enact and am. It is to reinterpret my life. To take new cognizance of my symptom, my difficulty, my trouble—whatever has brought me to therapy—is to reinterpret my life. It is done in and by (what we called in chapter 1) my second, or reflective, consciousness. However, some ways of taking cognizance are "growthful," while some ways are stultifying. We can describe this difference in terms of how my narrative, the framework of intelligibility for my everyday experience, accommodates the unintelligible element that is troubling me. We can also describe in this way the therapeutic task and at least one important class of resistances to it.

Which is more duplicitous: to allow symptoms, which are unintelligible, to become familiar and to acquire an established place as "my symptom," "my sickness," and so on, or to struggle with the ambiguities of who I really am, to examine what stories I find myself a part of, and to decide whether and how they can be and should be changed? Both the stultifying cognizance and the "growthful" cognizance are duplicitous; they both engage the doubleness of human consciousness of the world and reflective self-consciousness. But the content of their assessment, how they make things intelligible, is different.

In accepting the unintelligible into my life as my neurosis, thus making it intelligible, I am guided by that self-consciousness informed by popular psychology. For me to recognize my illness in this way is what (and who) I'm supposed to be, according to cultural themes and according to your, psychological, definition of me. That kind of owning a symptom occurs in and by my second consciousness.

Another motivational complex still accompanies this self-diagnostic one, but it is now submerged. My self-consciousness of struggling against something in the world becomes swamped by being conscious of having a symptom. I can forget my struggle with the world by focusing on myself. A psychological problem may then seem to be invading my life, like catching a disease, like a foreign element out of nowhere. This self-conscious duplicity, like the role of widow or unemployed, can be temporary and, during its stay, helpful in the face of confusion. In the longer run, this pretending can come to be a more nervous and delicate way of life, constantly alert to shore up the hiding from myself. As my anxiety about who I am becomes a mere symptom, I maneuver it so as to continue to avoid facing my problems in the world.

A second, more "growthful" cognizance of my symptom is also duplicitous. In struggling with the ambiguities of who I am, and in testing narratives for their fit and malleability, I make changes guided by a self-conscious desire to change, sometimes without knowing into whom I should change, thus tolerating ambiguity. Struggles inevitably engage cultural characters, or stereotypes, but these are also stand-ins for changes in who I have been. For example, if I should discover that I really am worthy of being loved, that may change everything. If I should come to believe that my sense that my parents did not find me loveable can be forgiven instead of endorsed, then I might experiment at being a self who impresses people well, and who finally, in fact, is loveable and loved.

Such a moment of growth combines my desire to be loved with a second consciousness of a self who is loveable, which in turn can guide my behavior so as to be perceived by others in exactly that way. I do not, in such a case, tell others to love me because my parents did not, or because I felt they did not. In fact, I may offer to love in the hope of being loved—a bit of duplicity that conceals a passive need behind an active one. I have, in such struggles, however, entered into culturally understood rituals, and I no longer settle for that intelligibility born of mere acceptance of the patient role.

KINDS OF DEPRESSION

Having understood the meaning of human lives in terms of narratives, we may now return to depression to see its implications. Pure depression, we recall, is not duplicitous. This contrasts with pseudodepression, in which one pretends to give up but continues the struggle duplicitously—secretly, while pretending not to. But there are still other kinds of depression. Depression, in its pure form, is giving up—a kind of surrender foreign to most lives. It can also be experienced as a posture of "I can't," which over time becomes also "I don't care that I can't." This in turn negates desire and moral injunction, as well as ability. There is no conflict in pure depression. Desire and moral injunction—and the struggle—have ceased. It is true, but fortunately quite rare, that a genuine and total human giving up, a surrender of all struggle, is possible.

Some depression, however, is a conflictual, struggling ordeal, neither the "I can't" of pure depression nor the pretendings of pseudodepression. Between these two lies agitated depression, where the conflicts between desires and moral injunctions, duties and fears, continue life's struggle. One's conflicts can include temptations to give up, alternating with rebellious refusal. Pure depression is adulterated in agitated depression by struggles that compromise the singular giving up of pure depression.[2]

Suppose my wife has left me, which, of course, would be awful and disorienting. I feel angry and hurt, but most of all I have an inexplicable sense that some other terrible thing is going to happen. I know my wife didn't really protect me from anything, not poverty, or even loneliness really, but her leaving seems to say that things are going rapidly downhill from here. My job feels in danger, my friends seem uneasy around me, and my pastimes now leave me cold and promise no pleasure. Am I condemned merely to sink lower and lower beneath the deterioration, the rusting, rotting ravages of time?

Initially, my feelings, let us suppose, were vivid:

I'm mad as hell that she would do this to me. Sometimes I imagine the creep who's living with her and I want to storm through their apartment, dumping out drawers, overturning tables, and smashing lamps. I'd get great pleasure out of finding them in bed, jerking off the covers, and spraying them with a fire extinguisher. I'd lift one end of the dresser and flip it over completely, smashing mirrors and perfume bottles on the way. I'd pull the drapes from their moorings and throw a chair into the window. And I'd leave feeling better.

But is it really her fault? If I had been a decent husband, she wouldn't have been looking, or even vulnerable, to his advances. I really blew it, and most of the time I had no idea I was blowing it. All those times she wanted my attention and I was just too busy doing something else. I have been a loser of a husband and I know it.

Even so, she didn't have to rub my nose in it like she did. She could have given me more warning, a chance to change, a little time to get myself into shape for her. She did threaten to leave, but how was I to know she meant it?

But no, she has definitively, and without concern for my feelings at all, simply gone on her way. I couldn't believe it, really. I'm left, here alone, face to face with my failure. No saving grace; no mitigating circumstances; nothing to represent all the things I did *right* through the years. All I have is a shambles of a life.

I don't deserve this. My marriage is gone and everything else has gotten shaky. I've lost my confidence; people now take advantage of me. I've become a weak sister. Nothing is safe.

But I'm not through yet. She wants to be friends. Absolutely not! I won't have anything to do with her. Sure, I'd like to get back at her, but I won't even do that. She doesn't deserve the privilege of my revenge.

Note that the anger, the revenge, and anxiety and even the guilt are not by themselves depressive. They are conflicted, perhaps, and struggling, surely. But they remain oriented toward a future. However, when they blend with the depressive potential of human personality, the capability to give up, they become less conflicted and more mired in the past; they become agitated depression.

A year later, the initial shock has become more depressed. The anger and hurt have been exhausted, and they have exhausted me. I have ceased being anxious about the progressive deterioration of my life and have become more resigned to it. The struggles about whose fault it is have disappeared; they are replaced by the growing conviction that I am simply a failure. My prideful refusal to have anything to do with the person whose leaving me caused all the trouble has become an apathy and a passivity. I am no longer indignant at injustices done, and I no longer struggle with whether I want or should generate a revenge. I have accepted the things that have happened, and also what I take to be their implications, namely, that I am not much good as a person after all.

I have not, however, given up. I have moments of determination: "All right, so I messed up my marriage; so I wasn't the greatest husband in the world. That doesn't mean I'm not good enough to walk down the street, to breathe the air, like everyone else. I'm not the only divorced man in the world. I've got my rights, and I can make my demands as well. I deserve the simple respect accorded human beings and I'll confront directly the person who'll not grant me that. The A&P cashier who isn't polite will get my contempt in exchange for hers. The neighbors who don't have the common decency to rake their leaves so they blow over on my lawn will hear from me too."

But such determination is spotty. I sometimes don't make my bed for weeks, and I drink every night to get to sleep. I wake up early and prowl around the house, occasionally sewing up cigarette burns on the upholstery or sweeping a floor, but usually I just cover such sights up and pretend they're not there. Or I don't even bother to pretend; I just accept them. During the early morning hours I occasionally have fantasies—strange and wonderful fantasies, such as the one that my house is under siege and I am protecting it from a well-organized, but finally inferior, force of invaders.

What has happened in the single year? Struggles with loss, with anger and anxiety, conflicted feelings of guilt and revenge have been drawn deeper and deeper into a funnel, the bottom of which is pure depression. This is the depressive potential of human personality. This situation bears closer examination. What makes the conflicts with desire and moral injunction into agitated depression instead of hopeful and anxious struggles? Depression in its pure form seems to attract these negativities, to pull them down to itself, so they become blended with and imbued with the flavor of depression, of death, of giving up and ceasing to care.

Somewhere in that new center of hopelessness lies guilt. I can become tempted to give up because I suspect that it is all my fault, that I am the guilty one, that the tragedy was caused by me, not her, or them, or anyone else but me—by whoever it was I thought I was being when I did this, then that, then the other thing, none of which helped, all of which made matters worse.

Depression, a potential of human personality, predates these struggles, and it predates the imitations of depression in pseudodepression. Depression seems to lie as an inherent counter pole to struggle and growth, much like death is the counter pole of life. *Struggle* is defined by the presence of hope and the absence of hopelessness, and *life* is defined by the presence of flourishing and, as far as I am concerned, indefinite postponement of death. In contrast to struggle, *giving up* is a boundary of human existence, imbedded in life's inherent shape, a boundary that is essential for life's vitality and freedom.

Depression is not, therefore, an accident that some people happen to fall into. It is slipping across that boundary of life into the giving up that surrenders the struggle. It is not merely accepting the abstract fact that death is possible; it is a giving in, not necessarily voluntary, but a recognition that I am mortal and mortality is me—a kind of reconciliation. Profound depression, seen only in mental hospitals, shows us persons whose will to struggle is simply exhausted. Indeed, human struggle is not inexhaustible. Giving up without dying is possible. It is not simply psychiatric. Such depression is essential, an inherent potential of human being. The language in terms of which we should understand it ought not be psychiatric. Such depression is human. The only language that can speak of it is ontological.

I am now saying that depression is a part of the inherent construction of human being. One does not observe such things, nor are they inferred. Such formulations come as a way to order our experience. The *disease model* of depression casts life and problem solving as normal and depression as a disease. But *giving up* is a possibility—not always a remote one, and never a completely absent one—a continuing and inherent possibility for human beings. Living life, its opposite, has to be chosen, although the choice seems simply to be common sense. Giving up is always an option.

The apparitions of depression I have dealt with are pretending to be depressed (or *pseudodepression*), *pure depression*, which is giving up, and the intermediate case of *agitated depression*. Each apparition approximates the essence, depression, in various ways and degrees. *Pure depression* brings us closest to that essence. Struggle has ceased; meaning has departed. It is very near to death. *Agitated depression* is struggle against having become depressed, having been drawn into the magnetic field of depression. One senses the essence of depression in agitated depression, but it is diluted by the continuing struggle, the continuing relevance of conflict, desire, moral injunction, by the continuing presence of meaning. *Pseudodepression* imitates that essence, reflects it as a theme in the process of doing something else, namely, struggling with loss and being anxious in one's pretentiousness.

We are ready now to summarize our understanding of depression by posing the following questions. (1) Why do I, in pseudodepression, pretend to be depressed? (2) Why, in agitated depression, do my struggles with desire and moral injunction, my postures of "I shouldn't" and "I won't" move from the anxiety of conflict to the depression of "I can't" and "I don't care?" (3) Why do I, in pure depression, give up? What is this "depressive potential of human personality?" Why is depression always a possibility? In terms of what kind of human nature does depression become intelligible?

MEANING AND DEPRESSION

The meaning of *human being*, as opposed to the meaning of a word, or event, or symbol, is a meaning in time. Something means something to *me* ultimately only if it fits into my life, which is a temporally flowing and developing network of meaning, in other words, a narrative, or story. I may find things meaningful in terms of static contexts of meaning, but I find these contexts meaningful in a human sense only by their role in my life, a temporally moving thicket of past-having-become-present-becoming-future.

There are many meaning systems, but they matter to me only in terms of the story that I am. The story I am is not, of course, separate from the story of my family, my nation, my world, but these all are merely narrative contexts of my particular, personal life. Narrative, then, is that temporally alive form of meaning that ultimately frames everything else. Human beings are storytellers, and their living enacts their stories creatively into the future.

The creation of meaning, a continual activity of the human subject, can therefore be specified as the continuing of an enactment of a narrative. The content of any person's narrative is in some ways given, and in some ways is created by that person. But in any case, it is a story one understands and knows that others understand as well.

Pseudodepression

We have said, in describing the pretending in depression, that I constrict the future by clinging to a fragment of the past or a role in the present and I also extravagate the future in denying an aspect of the past that I cannot face. This pretending in depression became, in our analysis, pretending to be depressed, or pseudodepression. Can we understand the pretending in depression and the pretending to be depressed in terms of creating a certain kind of narrative?

In adopting the role of bereaved, divorced, or unemployed, I borrow a story from the culture at large, and I fit myself into it, gladly, since my previous story has collapsed. I construe the events of my experience now as happening to a person I find intelligible, instead of one who is falling apart and chaotic. The purpose of this role and this story in the culture is to help individuals to buy some time to take up the tasks of re-inventing their future self and reaffirming their past selves. Those tasks are simultaneous and they are sad, longing for the now-gone past, and anxious, worried about the uncertain future.

But sometimes we fail to re-engage life. A person's motivation for keeping this role and the story beyond their time as a loan, is to continue to avoid that sadness and that anxiety. When this happens, the person avoids that sadness and anxiety by taking on another anxiety—that of pretending. Such pretending pretends my future is hopeless, that I am helpless, and that life means nothing to me anymore. This is a blatant pretense because my life has come to mean something quite definite; it is an enactment of the story of one who has suffered a loss and therefore is hopeless, helpless, and meaningless. This manifest hopelessness, helplessness, and meaninglessness are fraudulent in spite of their similarity to what I am avoiding. They are fraudulent because the story is not true: I am not hopeless, nor helpless, nor meaningless. I am, rather, unwilling to re-enter the rigors of life's story's openness to the future and boundedness to the past, unwilling to engage my own story with courage and faith. I am, therefore hoping to live without such rigors, I am helping myself do so by pretending.

These are, of course, very meaningful things to do. Their meaning has more to do with anxiety than one says, and it enacts more hope than one says. This pretending is not a self-conscious misrepresentation of myself to others, but it conceals from myself what exactly I am doing.

Indeed, in the conscious complexities of the experiences that leave me depressed, the marginal consciousness of my intentions to pretend, are not likely to come into focus. Indeed, they need do so only when I get beyond the borrowed time and adopt a more permanent role as "depressed."

I may have explained why people pretend to be depressed, but I haven't explained why people pretend to be depressed, instead of angry, or in love, or chronically sleepy. Well, people do pretend to be angry, in love, and chronically sleepy, but depression is a special kind of temptation. Pretending to be depressed is easy in the face of loss and sadness, not because I am facing that loss or sadness but rather because loss and sadness suggest, indeed, represent, that borderline situation at which human beings give up. Pseudodepression may not be real, but it is imitating something real and often very salient to human beings: The possibility of giving up.

We all have given up small projects in the face of adversity and that giving up is often rewarded by a tremendous relief—relief from the struggle, the energy drain, and the frustration of failure. We are acquainted with giving up on a small scale; we can imagine, and do imagine, giving up completely, letting go of all elements of our life stories and ceasing to be the author, actor, or observer of any creations in time at all. Suicide does this, often for this reason. Death generally is the occasion not only of anxiety but also of relief.

When I pretend to be depressed, I enact giving up without really doing so; I pretend to surrender on a much bigger scale than is the case. When I pretend to be depressed, I pretend that the border situation I give in to is death, for death is what makes depression possible and inevitable. Death surrounds life, and giving up surrounds engaging our stories vigorously. Death is, to be sure, a limit of human being, but it is not the only limit. There are other, smaller, less dramatic limits, such as our common bodily propensity for pain, our temporal propensity to lose, leave, and miss things, and our interpersonal propensity to fear rejection. These limits, the smaller insults of life, pretend in pseudodepression to be deathlike in their import. I respond as if I were giving in to the ultimate limit, death's drama and finality. But these smaller insults and limits are not like death, to which I must surrender. They limit me, but they do not demand my giving up on a large scale. Existentially, I am, in their challenge, challenged, not suffering the pretended role of real depression: hopelessness, helplessness, and meaninglessness.

It is not, of course, pretentious to feel sadness and to struggle with loss and with the task of redefining myself. The crucial question, in the face of life's depressing insults, is whether I accept the challenge or I pretend to give up. Very rarely, of course, do I really give up.

Pure Depression

We turn, now, to the real thing. Hopeless, helpless, and meaningless life is possible. Real giving up, pure depression, the utter surrender to death, but without dying, is a human possibility. In terms of the meaning-creating activities of the subject, pure depression is their *cessation*, a letting go of the rigors of life, the demands of the story, a surrender, in time, of time, after which there is no more time. It is an accepting of death, not in the vitalizing sense of appreciating how death configures life by bordering it and making it stand out, but rather in the sense of passively allowing it to swallow me up so that I simply disappear.

This possibility is known to us by way of analogy from smaller losses that are inevitable and permanent. It also is known to us in our consciousness of our own mortality, death. Why do human beings, who are still alive, give in to a small loss as if it were death? Why do people become patients? Let the loss overwhelm them? Why do they, we, give up? Is it simply a cosmic awareness of the vastness of the infinity that surrounds us, dwarfing everything, provoking us into the utmost humility? No, but this question, of the attractiveness of giving up, continues to matter for our psychology.

We shall argue that it is not a decision that is made independent of the social role allotted for just this purpose, and it is not made automatically, without the participation of our consciousness—a consciousness of self and all that being a self implies, such as knowing we are seen by others whose expectations permit, or even demand, certain behavior. Yet, giving all this up, pure depression, is possible. It is possible to surrender care about the world, about others, about being seen by others. Such giving up is like dying. No effort matters. All struggle surrenders. Life's burdens no longer provoke our effort. Pure depression is the human possibility to surrender human possibility. Nothing remains but actuality . . . and I just don't care about it.

Agitated Depression

Agitated depression is more serious than pseudodepression but still continues the resistance to giving up. It fights to retain a story that is in jeopardy, as if depression threatens to pull our struggles into the gaping abyss of nothingness. There is struggle in the agitation. In terms of the meaning-creating activities of the subject, this struggle is to sustain a story in the face of the possibility of giving up.

In my agitation, I am conflicted, between what I must but want not to do, but that struggle is also a struggle to retain a story, to remain a player in it, where the future is real and matters, and where I have a stake in what happens. Therefore, these struggles are also struggles between struggling and ceasing to struggle. In agitated depression, the stakes are that one could give up. In existential terms, the stakes are our being, not in the face of physical death, but fully in the face of that existential death of giving up, which we call pure depression. Agitated depression is depressive, but it is not only depressive. It is also desperate, courageous, heroic, even, in its resistance to nothingness.

DEPRESSIVE NARRATIVES

In order further to clarify the narratives of depression, we anticipate the next chapter by a brief look at the content of the narratives of depression. They invariably involve culpability. In the final analysis, our most difficult questions about depression must be answered in an exploration of guilt. But for now, let us note the drift toward fault in depressive narratives. The typical non-depressive narrative slants the facts, perhaps ever so slightly, in the direction of emphasizing virtues and minimizing faults. This directionality of bias is reversed in depressive narratives. The opposite bias is also a self-justification or a self-explanation, but one of a different sort.

When I say that my child's misbehavior is my fault, that my excessive debts reflect my own stupidity, and my current inability to sleep is because I am an inferior person, I have not only biased the facts, I have done so in a way to make myself intelligible to myself. My larger narrative will contain further such self-degradings. Something particular is going on in depressive narratives. That I am inferior to others who are superior, that I have failed, that I have sinned, that my life is stuck and going nowhere, that I really am alone, longing for love, but am unworthy of it—can we doubt that these themes make up a single package, well known to everyone in our culture as an attitude one can take, a possible interpretation of oneself? Can we doubt that this amounts to a well-known character in the cast of characters in modern Western societies? These are themes, already in our culture, that can be grafted on to any personal narrative, and can thereby lend further explanatory power to the narrative. It can make a confused life more intelligible.

Accepting these themes into the narrative of my life story changes things drastically. My graduating from high school becomes "they finally got rid of me" and even my joy of the moment becomes "I might be happy now, but wait 'til it's over—will I ever crash!" My future becomes bleak, a future of nothing changing, growing or developing. Hope recedes. As I indulge these themes, I am playing with, and playing at, giving up. I am imitating a pattern I know; I am pretending to lose my vitality; I am duplicitously trying to get through a confusing and anxious day or week or year by claiming that I cannot do so and, furthermore, that I don't care.

This duplicitous pretending is dangerous. It may well be an attitude I can strike to hold the line for a while in order to get some other things straightened out, but as a transformation of my whole narrative, it is an insidious infiltration of life by death, of vitality by decay, of energy by entropy. It puts me in danger of being sucked into an existential vortex, the force of which pulls me into the hopelessness I am playing with. In giving up, I allow the hopelessness to denude me of the duplicity with which I played, and it leaves me single-mindedly, unequivocally, sincerely, depressed. The quietude and peace of death appear to be attractive features of giving it all up, once and for all. The mystique of a macabre giving in to giving up can and does fascinate me. Its attraction lies in its simplicity—the alternative to duplicity, to complexity, to struggle and culture and anxiety and sadness—a final lack of ambiguity, of what I no longer want to face—the stuff of human life.

SUMMARY

In pretending to be depressed, I am enacting a cultural character that others can understand. But being myself in that way fails. In adopting the patient role, and allowing myself to be mentally ill, I construe the easy intelligibility of symptoms for that part of my narrative that is basically puzzling to me—my losses and my moods. It approaches a failure and, at a deeper level, it plays with what we use to make intelligible as surrender, and by the name "evil." Yet, pretending to be depressed, what we are calling pseudodepression, is not really agitated. Agitated depression toys more seriously with the possibility of giving up, but the agitation itself resists the giving up seen in pure depression even as it acknowledges such a possibility. That possibility is always there, of course.

As agitation exhausts itself, the giving up, pure depression, becomes a greater danger.

In pseudodepression, I threaten suicide, duplicitously, creating ambiguity about my sincerity (ambiguously pretending to pretend not to mean it). Such threats may be less than serious but nevertheless force us to struggle with them. This struggle can become agitated and, finally can undermine cultural agreements that are vital to social and personal life. Beyond that lies true giving up, which is not easy, but with the fatigue of agitation becomes easier. This sequence is one of sinking. Most clinical depression does not go all the way to pure depression, to genuine giving up of life.

Meanwhile, diagnosis by a professional is a cultural likelihood, necessitated, for example, by the prescription rule that antidepressant drugs require a diagnosis of depression. At the cultural and personal level, the diagnosis psychologizes my consciousness of my consciousness; indeed, it pathologizes it.

There are certainly cases where this fact has enhanced the force of the magnetic pull of our depressive potential—the always-present human possibility of truly and finally giving up.

CHAPTER FIVE

─── ───

Loss, Anger, Fear, Longing, and Guilt

FALSE CAUSES OF DEPRESSION

I have stated that depression is a major human alternative. Pure depression is like dying insofar as those who suffer from it surrender the struggles of living, even though they do not cease to live. It is also like dying in that it can happen any time, with little or no effort, only passive acceptance. People can always become depressed, and when they do, others find it at once paradoxical and comprehensible. Death in life is paradoxical, but then again, depression is a "mental illness."

Further, depression is related to a fundamental constituent structure of human being—our guilt—the power of which can lead us to negate life itself, if we do not otherwise deal with it. Dealing with our guilt is much the same as dealing with human evil.

This understanding of depression most distinctly does not say that depression comes from loss, anger, fear, or longing. It does come from guilt, but guilt has to be understood as an ontological phenomenon, as built into the structure of human beings, not as a psychological phenomenon created by parents, nor as an evolutionary phenomenon created by culture. We shall discuss guilt in chapters 6 and 8.

Loss

Loss is commonly said to lead to, or to precipitate, depression.[1] I believe that loss confuses me, that in my confusion I become anxious, and in that anxiety I seek some posture or attitude, some role or character that will make my self intelligible to myself. The experience of loss is an experience of emptiness. Something or someone is missing. In its place is nothing. That nothing can come to feel like the whole world; that absence can spread its vacuity throughout everything and leave me denuded in my attempt to cope. How can I deal with loss?

In the short run, grieving and mourning are both permitted and encouraged. We have many social rituals that ensure sufficient opportunity for experiencing this emptiness, protesting it, and beginning the process of rebuilding. Sometimes the echoes of the loss make this a protracted process, and sometimes we go to psychiatrists for help. They tell us that "being depressed" is a natural way of dealing with loss.

However, being depressed is also a posture, an attitude, role, or character, which can substitute for working through the meanings of a loss such as the death of a loved one. When this happens, it is not genuine depression, not really giving up. It is, rather, pretending to be depressed, an anxious activity that uses the themes and style of depression as a way of coping with the confusion, anxiety, and emptiness of loss.

The themes and style of depression are used because depression is a vivid possibility for human beings; we all know we can give up. I know further that doing so presents a certain face to others and to my own reflections. My reaction to loss is rarely giving up. More commonly, I wear the depressive face as a way to continue, rather than to quit, the struggle of life. Thus, I do not give up; my agitation may be dramatic, but it, too, is not giving up—it is, rather, the opposite of giving up.

Anger

Anger is commonly said to lead to, or to precipitate, depression. In fact, depression is commonly said to be nothing but anger turned back against the self.[2] In an evolutionary view, anger is an adaptive response to frustrations of various kinds, but it is decidedly dangerous for those species whose members are intensely interdependent, such as human beings.

In such species, a second reaction to frustration, following anger and negating it, is depression, which is more adaptive in an interdependent community. It provokes sympathy, perhaps, but more importantly, it clearly protects the community and the individual from the frustrated expression of anger.[3] It is, also, a possibility for those organisms complex enough to control their instinctual discharge through directing it back on themselves. Again, human beings are the best, but probably not the only, example.

I know that I can turn anger back against myself, which is a way to prevent its direct expression, a way to prevent retaliation from others by enacting that retaliation myself ahead of time, as it were, and also a way to provoke others into giving me what I want. All of these phenomena are real, impressive, even dangerous in their clinical extremes. But they are not depression.

The guilt seen in depression comes from the ontological essence of human being, not from anger turned back against myself. That guilt may be laced with anger, or even become violent in suicide or some other self-punitive behavior, and anger turned back against myself may make the violence possible. But neither the guilt, nor the depression, are violent or angry. It is important to let guilt and depression be guilt and depression, not some modified form of anger.

Fear

Depression also has been explained as a by-product of fear. Depression paralyzes me, prevents me from venturing back into the fray. It translates discouragement into inaction, lethargy, and apathy, all of which ensure that whatever discouraged me—failure, inferiority, disappointment—won't have to be faced again. In other words, depression serves my fear of a repetition of these events; it protects me from what I fear by keeping me out of the regions of risk.[4]

I have no doubt that fear can result in paralysis, that I can, in such circumstances, call myself depressed, and that this self-labeling not only makes myself intelligible, as in pretending to be depressed after a loss, but also it protects me from admitting and experiencing the fear. But this is not depression. It is again a pretending, a taking over of a reaction not because I have given up, but because this seeming to give up is a way of continuing the struggle, to protect myself and to maximize my gains with minimum risk. Again, the depressive themes and style of giving up are available and used, but their use in this way is not the genuine giving up of depression.

Longing

People who are depressed certainly seem to be dominated by their longing. When I am depressed, my longing knows no bounds. It is combined with suspicions or convictions that I am unworthy of the love I so desperately need, and so it is hopeless. In enacting these suspicions or convictions, I provoke reassurances and even disproofs from others. I coerce them into correcting my too harsh self-judgment, reaping praise and, most of all, love. Depression, it seems, is driven by longing and strives to provoke sympathy and love as a satisfaction of its drive.[5]

Again, I may express my longing in this way, and it may have these effects. Doing so may also express depressive themes and imitate a depressive style. But the forward-looking, hopeful striving for a gratification of my longing—even as I may look and sound hopeless and helpless—is quite the opposite from the giving up of depression.

TRADITIONAL VIEWS OF THE CAUSE OF DEPRESSION

It appears, then, that loss, anger, fear, and longing all motivate behavior that seems depressive but is not. Anxiety, anger, fear, and longing are all quite definite ways of being in the world, each quite distinct from depression. Depression, I am arguing, comes from guilt.[6]

Why, then, do these feelings eventuate in apparent depression? There are two answers, or two kinds of answers, to this question. First, the depressive themes and style that I imitate in the face of these exigencies work, they yield me a psychological gain; they are gratifying in their effects on others. But, they also work to protect me from experiencing the primary affect, even as they express indirectly such affects as anger or fear. This indirect expression is another kind of gratification, and it is one that we do not need to take responsibility for if we appear depressed.

Why is depression so available, so well known, so popular? Aside from its efficacy, depression is known to us because it is a universal possibility of all human beings. I always can give up, and indeed, I am not infrequently tempted to do so. At the boundaries of ordinary life is death—a horrifying prospect, but also a peaceful one. Death is attractive for its anesthesia. If only it didn't end life. If only I could die and yet not close out the future completely.

There is, it turns out, a way to do just that, which is to withdraw into what professionals call depression. Indeed, our professional diagnostic practice, urged on by the marketing of antidepressant medication, may be the most recent and most powerful factor in keeping the depressive option open and popular.

At the edge of ordinary life, therefore, lies depression as a constant alternative, a rarely used one in its pure form, but a frequently imitated one. We know it also for its guilt—a well-known human affect that not only punishes us but also, since we were children, protects us from punishment. Again, depression, like our essential guilt, is built into human being. It is giving up—an ontological possibility; it is a human alternative, and it is frequently indulged strategically.[7]

Freud's Theory of Guilt

I have made three assumptions about guilt for most of my professional life. First, guilt is, I have long assumed, anger turned back against myself. Second, I have assumed that I learned to feel guilty from being punished by my parents. Third, guilt is, therefore, internalized parental punishment. I do what parents did, express anger at that child I call "myself." This explains the behavior of self-punishment and its accompanying feeling—guilt.

The guilt feelings are covert self-punishment, which motivate ritualistic or fantastic compensatory behavior or substitutes for such behavior that make me suffer. Put another way, I have always assumed that self-punitive behavior is really designed both to express and relieve my self-punitive feeling of guilt.

All of this is Freudian. Freud's was the first psychology I learned, and I learned it before I appreciated that every psychology is based on an ontology. I knew that Sigmund Freud was a Darwinian and that Darwinism often replaces a more explicit ontology. But I did not conclude that I might disagree with Freud about such things as guilt because his theory seemed to explain so much, so well. Even now, questioning it seems to put at risk a certain security I have always derived from thinking I know what is going on.

Freud didn't formalize his ideas about guilt until the 1920s, so it is really Freud's logically first thesis, not his chronologically first. His first thesis, which became my first assumption, was that guilt is really anger turned back against myself. The idea behind this interpretation of guilt is that anger is more basic, more given in human nature, than guilt, which is really only a derivative of anger. Anger directed outward is hate; anger directed inward is self-hate, or guilt. Anger directed outward leads to aggression; anger directed inward leads to aggression against myself, or self-punishment.

Behind this idea, in turn, lies Freud's instinct theory, which states that aggression, along with sex, is selected for in the Darwinian processes of evolution. Those organisms with stronger sex drives reproduce more than those with weaker sex drives, perpetuating strong sex, eliminating weak sex, selecting, as it were for the heartiest sexuality. Similarly, those organisms with more aggression survive to reproduce more, while those with less aggression survived less, reproduced less, and, hence, were selected against. Just as sex was selected for, ensuring the survival of the genetic line, so was aggression selected for, ensuring the survival of the individual organism so that it could reproduce. Sociobiologists extend this logic into an explanation for almost everything.

What is portrayed here is what Herbert Spencer called a struggle for "the survival of the fittest," a phrase also central to the later 19th-century Social Darwinism of Spencer, Lester Ward, Henry Ward Beecher, and Andrew Carnegie, which justified the capitalist system as a "natural" arena of struggle and the amassing of great fortunes as reward to persons naturally "most fit." The biological vision of Darwin is reproduced in the social vision of Spencer (actually, it's much older, going back to Thomas Malthus and before him Thomas Hobbes), amounting to a cosmology and, finally, to an ontology of human being.

These ideas were totally consistent with, perhaps we can say they underlie, Freud's psychology, which leads to the second assumption about guilt that I reject, namely, that guilt is learned from parents, particularly from being punished by parents. I recall slapping my son's hand one evening for playing with a lamp cord. The lamp cord was almost a nightly routine when he was about two years old. A few days later, I observed my son as he began to play with the lamp cord. He stopped abruptly, saying to himself what I had said, "No! Do *not* play with the lamp cord." He, then, slapped his own hand. It was a vivid example of a prohibition, originating from the outside, coming to be internalized.

Freud argued that not only the prohibition but also an enduring image of the punitive parent is internalized and becomes that little voice of conscience. It is my voice, now internalized by my son with which my son struggles before a transgression, and under whose condemnation he suffers after. The internal dynamics of our personalities reproduce the family setting within which we learned our most basic lessons about life and truth, love, hate, guilt, and pride.

This psychology cannot be all wrong. So much of our adult lives does recapitulate the dynamics of the primary family that it seems obvious that the fundamental human relationship is parent-child. It also seems obvious that other kinds of relationships are derivative from that basic, hierarchical, dominance relationship, which is embedded in the primary family and in the earliest and deepest layers of our psyches.

In the family situation, as opposed to the individual situation, guilt involves the transformation of anger into self-punishment. The fittest individual is not tested alone, but rather embedded in a social group where individuals work together to survive. Therefore, one's ability to work cooperatively depends on basic learning within the primary family, where an individual is not simply an individual but becomes a loyal family member, whose selfish desires are tempered by this loyalty and punished, first by the parents, and later by oneself. Guilt is, therefore, necessary. It is a requirement; the price we pay, Freud said, for the very existence of social life—of civilization.

Understood this way, guilt exists only as a part of a hierarchical or dominance situation. My experience of guilt is really an experience of punishment for having broken a rule laid down by a dominant parent (or some other authority). A civilization without dominance, where virtually everyone, including children, is equal, could not be one of peace, because it could not be one of guilt. Guilt requires the situation within which it was learned—hierarchy. Hobbes also believed this; John Locke and Immanual Kant did not.

Thus, a major interpretation of life in the Western world is that guilt necessarily involves authority. It is learned in the authority situation of the family, and it recapitulates those feelings, which in turn recreate that hierarchical situation in adult social life. Social authority, therefore, becomes both possible and necessary. That is, social order, domination by virtue of consent, and the acknowledged right to dominate become possible. Sheer power becomes the more socialized, legitimate "authority." Social life, therefore, with respect for law, for the state, for the right of government to define correct behavior, is possible, but it depends, in this view, on children having grown up in families.

The experience of guilt in a religious context, too, depends on the presence of an authority, God, in whose eyes, and in the light of whose laws, one has sinned. Were it not for God, Feodor Dostoevsky tells us, all things would be possible. Freud is not the only one to notice that the relation of man to God recreates the relation of child to parent. The most startling conclusion from that is not, as Freud thought, that God is a mere psychic projection from our childhood.

More important here is the proposition that we adults, who graduate from the authority of our parents, necessarily recreate that authority situation in our cosmology. We believe in a God. Further, we need to do this in order to shore up our morality, or sociality—in a word, our capacity to feel guilt. In this view, guilt is impossible without authority.

I want to argue that this view is not the whole story. Guilt can be, and often is, created by punishment by authority, but that is not the only way it is created, nor is it necessarily the most basic way. In addition, guilt created in this way is not the most basic guilt. There is another way to create guilt—we might call it the Jewish mother technique. For example, suppose someone named Leonard Cohen decides to eat with his girlfriend instead of coming home for supper one night. He is twenty years old, and he dutifully calls his mother to tell her his plans. His mother reacts badly: "It's okay. Why should you want to eat with your old and ugly mother. She's not a good cook anyway. And the steak, it's kosher but it's not as good as what you'll get in a restaurant. I'll give it to the dog. Here Major! Here! Have some steak! We *were* going to eat it, but Lenny has decided he doesn't want to eat with us. It's good, isn't it, Major? Lenny, can you hear? Here, I'll hold the phone down so you can hear the dog enjoy the steak I bought for you."

What Lenny's mother is doing is what we all do sometimes. We display our suffering for another to see, presumably for that other who is causing the suffering. This makes the other feel guilty; it has a better than even chance, depending on one's technique, of getting the other to change his or her behavior.[8]

It is hard to believe that Freud did not have a Jewish mother. It's also hard to believe Freud was not familiar with this way of evoking guilt. He surely was familiar with it, but he did not consider it basic. For Freud, the instincts were more basic. He saw guilt as anger—instinctual energy—turned back on the self. Therefore, the human socialization of biological instincts, punishment in the family, is where guilt comes from. For Freud, then, that is the basic definition of guilt.

The notion that guilt can also be evoked by the suffering of another was incidental to Freud; this fact did not signal to him anything about its basic nature. Its instinctual and developmental origin described its nature. Guilt derives from authority no less than it derives from anger, in Freud's view. In both cases, guilt is a derivative phenomenon, universal perhaps, but not ontologically given.

The third assumption, that guilt is self-punishment, follows easily from the first two, that guilt is anger directed back on myself and that guilt was learned in, and always, therefore recapitulates, an authority situation. To the biology of Darwin and the sociology of Spencer, we add the psychology of Freud, which is developmental and familial, and the cosmology of the Judeo-Christian tradition, or at least the main stream of it, where God is authority over all.

These various origins may contradict one another at many points, but they fit together nicely into an interpretation of guilt. It is certainly not easy to dismiss the power of this interpretation, for it shapes our understanding at such basic levels that any other interpretation would seem *not* to understand the most obvious facts of life, which are given to us clearly by Darwin, Freud, sociobiologist E. O. Wilson, religious authorities everywhere, and, of course, by common sense.

An Alternate Interpretation

What if guilt is not as I have always assumed it to be? What if guilt is not anger directed back at myself, but rather is something other than self-hate? That would not be to say that there isn't self-hate; it merely says that guilt is something else that shouldn't be confused with self-hate. What if guilt is not learned in the primary family? What if it comes from somewhere else?

If guilt does come from somewhere, that would not deny that basic things are learned in the primary family, including fear of punishment and respect for authority. But as dependent as respect for authority may be on familial fear of punishment, which in turn is learned from one's parents, these authority relations are not the same thing as guilt, and they should not be confused with it.

If guilt is not self-hate, then what is it? If guilt does not come from being punished, then where does it come from? Guilt is an experience whose qualities are not reducible to something else like anger or hate. The experience of guilt includes a cognitive recognition of having hurt someone and an affective flavor or sadness, sorrow, or remorse, but it is not a compound made up of such elements.

Because of his instinct theory, Freud saw depression as merely introverted anger. But this misses a crucial point. Rather, depression, as connected to guilt the way it is interpreted here, is an "originary" experience of acknowledging, with a feeling of sorrow, having hurt a person.[9]

Guilt is aversive, but our reactions to the aversion, such as the desire to make amends, to do penance, to be forgiven, and to think of something else—these reactions are not guilt. Like self-punishment, they may be guilty, or they may be self-hating, for that matter, but they are derivative, not "originary." For most people, having hurt another person is as profound an experience as any.

The basic format of guilt involves, then, myself and another I have hurt, not a rule I have broken or an authority I have offended. Guilt depends on my ability to take the role of the other, imaginatively to feel his or her hurt, while simultaneously acknowledging I am responsible for that hurt.

The self-other format, where I can vicariously experience the other's experience and know he or she can vicariously experience mine, is native to human beings and is as basic to our nature as authority relations. It is as necessary to civilization, from family life to the state, as punishment, fear of punishment, assertion of and respect for authority.

It is learned, in a way, for the earliest experiences of our lives shape it and give it content. But it is also inherent. Subhuman species seem to have notably less of such capability; most have none at all. Authority relations are one version of this learned sociality; fear is an emotion and punishment is an event we all learn very early. But authority relations are not made up of only fear; they are accompanied by gratuitous generosity and love. Furthermore, parents, in particular, become, by the time a child is three or four, a distinct version of "person," like myself, only bigger, wiser, stronger.

When the self-other capabilities of a child are limited to fear of authority and not balanced with love, then we see one distinct form of psychopathology. But when guilt is also missing, then we see another, more serious, pathology, not only of individuals but also sometimes of large groups.[10]

But what about self-punishment, as a fact? Does it not occur? Does it not in turn derive from having been punished? Does not that derivation lead us to respect authority? Yes, to all these questions. But are these actually the stuff out of which guilt is made? This is the central question of this section.

I believe that much of the associative content of genuine guilt is learned in the presence of authority, for that is how we grow up. But origins of when and where to feel guilt do not define the essence of guilt. My walking emerged from having crawled, having pulled myself up, having bounced, having staggered, lurched, fallen and tried again. Yet my walking is not defined by, nor made up of, crawling, bouncing, and lurching. It is a new Gestalt, not given at birth but no less inherent in my nature than my upright posture, and no more inherent in my nature than my conscience.

In the 1930s, Gordon Allport (1937) proposed his theory of "functional autonomy." A motive, say, to be a lawyer, may be historically related to one's desire to convict one's father of fantasy crimes, but his relationship is merely historical. Its origin is not still in its center. Functionally, the motive to be a lawyer is autonomous from these origins, having found motive enough in the study of law, the making of money, and power to control events or further the cause of justice.

The father's fantasized crimes are no longer what the lawyer is doing as he practices his trade. These meanings of his trade have become peripheral to new centers as his personality has grown and matured. At the very least, I am claiming that the fear of punishment and respect for authority are similarly displaced from the center of guilt as personality evolves. They may be historically related to guilt, but guilt is functionally autonomous of its origins.

Perhaps it is the case that in the healthy person, guilt is functionally autonomous of its origins, whereas in the less mature person, it is not. Less mature persons may still be authority-bound, or merely self-punitive. Mature guilt graduates from these origins while immature guilt does not. This view is similar to that of Lawrence Kohlberg (1963) and William Perry (1981), where "maturity" is reckoned according to a sequence of developmental stages.

However, Allport, Kohlberg, and Perry fall short of an understanding of guilt as ontologically given. To say that guilt is ontologically given is to say that the very being of humans is structured in such a way that guilt occurs. It is not only different from anger or fear of authority; it is a fundamental element.

Guilt is a universal human experience that, like the ability to reckon reality dispassionately, may in any given case be distorted, defective, or limited to self-hate or authority situations. But in most settings, the basic shape of human being shows the more essentially human experience of guilt as guilt.[11]

This formulation also implies that when I feel guilty, I am engaging a fundamental structure of human being. This is different from engaging my history of authority relations and punishment relations with my parents and different from engaging my anger grounded in a biologically given instinct, although these historical and biological factors were crucial to my development.

Freud's theory of superego might be said to be no less a description of a second consciousness than the one contained in this essay. However, according to Freud's theory, the superego's origin exhausts its content; morality is defined as the attitudes and rules of one's models with whom one has identified. Not only is conscience probably more than this, the second consciousness is more than a watchdog "over-me" or superego. Its other features will be noted and elaborated upon presently.

To say that guilt is ontological is to say something different from Freudian theory, but it is not to say that what Freud thought has no ontological meaning. Myself *as* my history, *of* these relations, *through* the instincts of sex and aggression exhausts the ontology of the self according to Freud.

To say that guilt is ontological, as we are now doing, is to affirm a different ontology from Freud's ontology. It is to argue that guilt is just as basic to human nature as anger and aggression. It is not merely developmentally created, but rather is ontologically given—that I acknowledge, through the feeling of sadness, having hurt another.

Guilt happens not because of my history, my family, or my development, but rather simply because it is human to do so. Human beings vicariously feel the feelings they see in others, and know how, say, pain or insult or sorrow feels. When we cause that experience in others, we feel guilty. It is a rare and remarkable deviation from normal humanity for guilt to be absent.

SUMMARY

I have said that guilt is acknowledging, with a feeling of regret and sadness, that I have hurt someone. I have said that it is a basic human experience, not merely derived from anger (as in self-aggression) or authority (as in fear of punishment), although both of those feelings are real and easily confused with guilt, or even mixed with them in any given case. Finally, I have claimed that guilt is as fundamental to human experience as the capability to experience the pain of another person vicariously—a fundamental human capability, indeed.

I have not, however, really explained why knowing I have hurt another, whose pain I vicariously feel, should make me feel guilty. In order to do that, we shall have to look again at evil, a topic that has already come up twice, but not very fully.

I argue in the next chapter, with the help of the philosopher Paul Ricoeur, that guilt lies at the root of depression rather than the anger, fear, and authority mentioned in this chapter. What is the meaning of such a claim? What is at stake here? To be sure, the depth of this issue is not immediately visible. Let us think it through once again.

We are accustomed to thinking of depression as anger turned back on oneself. This was Karl Abraham's and Freud's starting point, and it seems so sensible that to disagree is to seem to deny the obvious. Guilt is also laced with introverted anger, and so guilt and depression are closely related.

To argue that depression and guilt are closely related (agreeing with Freud) and that both are unrelated to anger (disagreeing with Freud) may seem to be splitting theoretical hairs. What do I experience when I'm depressed? What affects are involved, and how are they directed? The question seems answerable, and yet I realize as well that to claim that depression comes from guilt and not from anger is to make a claim that is seemingly beyond verification. I am not sure at all how one could settle this question, and I am reminded of William James's remarks about the psychology of his day and its efforts to deal with emotions:

I may have been surfeited by too much reading of classical works on the subject, but I should as lief read verbal descriptions of the shapes of the rocks on a New Hampshire farm as toil through them again. They give one nowhere a central point of view, or a deductive or generative principle . . . They distinguish and refine and specify *in infinitum* without ever getting on to another logical level. Whereas the beauty of all truly scientific work is to get to ever deeper levels . . . Is there no way out from this level of individual description in the case of the emotions? I believe there is a way out, but I fear few will take it. (1890, Vol. II, 1890, 448–449)

We shall not take James's way out—at least not exactly—but perhaps we ought to take note of this plea to get to another logical level. It may be the case, as James suggests, that phenomenological descriptions of emotional states, unattached to the contexts in which they are experienced, will simply result in "one of the most tedious parts of psychology."

The context to attend to, contrary to James's focus on visceral sensations, is the situation of the experiencing person—what is before me now, what I remember, anticipate, and how I put it all together into a coherent, meaningful experience. That is, when I am depressed, am I angry? Guilty? Sad? All of the above? The names, of emotional states, apart from a context of a living person in a meaningful situation, do not name what we must name in order to understand depression. They are on the wrong logical level.

Being depressed, then, is not to be defined as some version of being angry, guilty, or sad, but rather as some version of being-in-the-world, such as being lonely, having been rejected or abandoned, having failed in one's endeavors or obligations. This level of description gets at a human situation, not a psychic state or a mood.

Guilt, as I shall describe it, is really less a psychic state than it is a human situation. If I claim that depression comes from guilt rather than anger turned inward, I am not saying it comes from one emotional state rather than another. I am saying instead that it comes from one kind of human situation rather than another. Those human situations that at once anger me and prohibit the outward expression of my anger are different from those human situations where I have failed to live up to the demands of an ethical or moral ideal that bears on me. The former situations are upsetting, without a doubt and can lead to impressive irrationalities.

But to the extent that these irrationalities look like depression, they are, to that extent, pretending. For depression, pure depression unadulterated by pretending to be depressed, comes from situations of having failed to live up to my moral standards. In the extreme, one can, in fact, give up. Giving up is a more profound human possibility than anger.

Now this claim may, at first, seem no more verifiable than the claim about emotional states. Indeed, it could reduce to a mere matter of definition. It is possible to specify as follows: If the situation within which the depression is experienced is angering yet blocks the outward expression of that anger, then we are looking at pseudodepression. If, on the other hand, it is a moral failure, then we are looking at true depression.

But wait. These are trivial criteria, whereas the human situation of guilt is not. I am almost in agreement with O. Hobart Mowrer (1967) that "the main reason mental illness has been such a mystery in our time is that we have so assiduously separated it from the realm of personal morality and immorality" (vii)—almost in agreement, but not quite. There are many reasons why we don't understand "mental illness," and I do not mean quite the same thing as Mowrer does by "morality." But to spell that out, we shall have to turn to the next chapter.[12]

CHAPTER SIX

Psychotherapy, Psychopharmacology, and Pretending

PSYCHOPHARMACOLOGICAL TREATMENT

Drug treatment is the first line of medical response to depression. In fact, insofar as family doctors are concerned, this is the only response. Increasingly, this is true of psychiatrists as well. Psychotherapy, an earlier approach still often used, aims to enable the depressed person to understand the reason for her or his feelings, and to find a way to deal with them less painfully. However, this process is time-consuming and personally demanding on the part of both patient and therapist, and it is increasingly being accompanied by, if not simply replaced by, psychopharmacology—that is, drug therapy.

It is hard to tell the future, but a number of circumstances favor drug therapy. It is much quicker and, thus, less expensive, and insofar as therapy is increasingly paid for by insurance companies, they prefer, or even in some cases insist on, drug therapy. Advertising increasingly in popular magazines, pharmaceutical corporations are slowly persuading the public to ask for drug therapy as well.

How far will this trend go? Will psychotherapy disappear? Will more and more people use drugs? Will a time come when virtually everyone will be taking some pill or other to help them get through the day? This trend, which began in the mid 20th century, has been increasing steadily and shows no signs of slowing down (Keen, 1998). It is worth asking what could curb, if not reverse, the tendency of human beings to augment their capability for happiness chemically—without the hang-overs attending alcohol.

A Historical Analogy

Karl Polanyi, in *The Great Transformation* (1957), describes the painful evolution from a pre-industrial and pre-capitalist society to the industrial capitalism of modern Europe. Most of this change took place in the 19th century. In the 20th century, the resulting material well-being of much of the West has existed side by side with enormous class struggle and injustice.

In his introduction to Polanyi's book, R. M. MacIver credits Polanyi with the insight that the major players in the 19th-century struggle did not always see the options clearly. Many thought the development of industry could be controlled, or even stopped, if only we would try.

Some advocated a quick return to the 18th century, a pre-industrial past, as if that were only a matter of popular will. The voices of progress, on the other hand, envisioned what has become the 20th century's freedoms—of enterprise, of speech, of labor, of the market economy—the most important one of which is the freedom to try to produce ourselves into happiness.

This polarity, between reactionaries and visionaries, has perhaps been neglected among 20th-century formulations of modernity and its history. For by the late 19th century, industrialization was clearly inevitable, and it contained within itself another, pre-emptory polarity, that of the more egalitarian Marxist industrialization versus the more elitist capital control and profit taking. But the earlier question of either progress (toward industrialization) or regress (to feudalism) will concern us in this account.

In thinking about depression, it is impossible not to think about anti-depressant medications. Wellbutrin was advertised on television; Prozac was made famous, and stylish, by Peter Kramer. An entirely new vocabulary of the accoutrements of depression has appeared—"tricyclic antidepressant medication," "selective serotonin reuptake inhibitors."

Like industrialization, psychopharmacology affects everyone. Both are like the electrification of our lives a century ago. Electricity and industrialization had opponents who disappeared with time. Psychopharmacology, like electricity and industry, changes our experience so basically that unaltered consciousness may come to seem quaint and rustic but essentially irrelevant to human life. Like living without electricity, not controlling human consciousness chemically may become a picturesque snapshot of a barely remembered past.

MacIver does not think either of the two 19th-century postures he describes, "progress" (toward industrialization) or "regress" (to feudalism), makes sense in retrospect, regardless of how obvious they may have seemed at the time. Advocacy among those who cared mattered less than the simple momentum of technology and science in making life better. Therefore, "What our age needs," according to MacIver, was and is neither the security of feudal remnants, nor the unleashing of human productive power. Rather we needed then and we need now "the reaffirmation for its own conditions and for its own needs, the essential values of human life" (x).

Indeed, pre-industrial society cannot return. In carving out a future, we must reinvent "the essential values of human life" and find a way to actualize them in an age that is saturated with produced goods and is irreversibly industry dependent.

Is there a parallel evolution in the struggle to envision "life after psychopharmacology?" It appears that this technological achievement of the 20th century is here to stay. In half a century of psychiatric practice, there have been moments of hesitation, but the overall trend is unequivocally to practice psychiatry by practicing pharmacology. Psychotropic drugs are the first line treatment for nearly every diagnosis, for most psychiatrists, and perhaps for all institutionalized patients.

Drug therapy appears to offer a liberation from enormously difficult psychological strains, as well as from less difficult, but still painful and inconvenient, moods and anxieties. Perhaps, like remembering pre-industrial culture, remembering non-pharmacologically improved life will be merely sentimental. For the vast majority of psychiatric patients, and for many others who simply ask their doctors for drugs, non-pharmacologically improved consciousness is becoming a mere memory, and often a painful one.

Perhaps we are wasting our time idealizing pre-pharmacized consciousness, for it is no more possible than pre-industrial culture. Perhaps naked human experience, unclothed by chemical treatment, is analogous to occasional walks in the park, retreats to the cabin, and other escapes to remnants of pre-technological nature.

Perhaps we need a concerted effort to see clearly, before non-pharmacized consciousness retreats to a marginal status, "the essential values of human life" so as to ensure their presence and their flourishing even in post-pharmacized consciousness.

Let us, in other words, be clear about what aspects of consciousness we do not want sacrificed to the technology of psychiatry, to the ideologies of those who control our children with drugs, or to the temptations created by corporate sales pitches, such as "Depression Hurts; Prozac Can Help" (Ely Lilly advertisement). While we may all, in a generation or so, be taking something chemical to improve human consciousness, let us not be completely and mindlessly taken in by those who promise us that life is better with pills.

A 21st-century protest against psychochemical manipulation may be as vain as the 19th-century protest against industrialization. The pre-pharmacized consciousness may be no more within our reach than the pre-industrial culture was in the 19th century. Remembering may be important, but it can be misleading if it becomes the definer of our goals.

To recall, and perhaps to idealize, the ways anxiety, depression, and even hallucination enriched our pre-pharmacized consciousness is less germane than to be clear as to how our central values can have a continued presence even in the absence of pristine, purely natural human experience.

It must be said that part of my suspicion and alarm at the incredible growth of psychopharmacological therapy comes from my professional dismay that its predecessor, psychotherapy, may be replaced entirely. In reflecting on this question, it is relevant that psychotherapy, with its conversational, dialectical pattern, permits no prediction; it is more an art than a science.

Should this therapeutic wandering around and through consciousness survive instead of pharmacological focusing on symptom removal? We ought perhaps to be less alarmed and more exploratory about what is at stake and what should be preserved. It is easy to be either sentimental or hardheaded and "realistic," but it is not always easy to tell the difference.

So sacred have become the back roads and villages of psychotherapy, especially perhaps to its practitioners, that the superhighways and shopping malls of psychopharmacology sometimes seem an abomination. Yet, our reflection must consider that drugs make depression and anxiety disappear more efficiently with every generation of pharmaceutical refinement.

But depression and anxiety are about something in life that needs attention. No amount of convenience and efficiency in eliminating them replaces the importance of listening to them. Depression and anxiety often tell us of the sadness and the fear of traditional intricacies of obligation, of ambiguities about who we should become—the back roads and villages that are a part of our lives. Of course, these obligations and ambiguities are not the whole of anyone's life. Superhighways and shopping malls are my life too. I may pronounce unfavorable judgments on the quality of highways and malls as "life," but all of us are also shoppers and travelers, and we have not ceased, therefore, to be human beings.

We must certainly agree that some things are lost and some things are gained. History moves. But neither loud protest nor mere resignation is an adequate response to the fact that, like electricity, psychoactive chemicals are becoming some part of everyone's life. Even if I don't take them myself, I deal with those who do, and thus, we are all affected. As Woody Guthrie has informed us: "Times are a-changin'" and we have a stake in the change.

We preserve bits of the past because they are valuable. Much that is valuable may be lost, but some, perhaps sometimes the best, is saved. What exactly from the world of back roads and villages do we want to preserve amidst the rather more salient quick fixes for human distress available in a drugstore?

PRESERVING VALUES

John Kekes (1988) reflects on the life of Michel de Montaigne, whose political service and intense personal reflection embodied the usual nexus of conflict between public identity and private experience. Duty to his political life and practical tasks of leadership were in constant conflict with self-exploration, independent judgment, and inner integrity.

While Montaigne was a 16th-century mayor of Bordeaux, thus engaging the intense intercultural conflict of Renaissance politics, this aspect of his life was not all that different from what we now, living in 21st-century industrial, democratic society, call "responsible." That is, the qualities of mind, then and now, that facilitate good living are strikingly similar, thus justifying Kekes's close attention to this particular life.

Self-exploration and self-direction amidst turbulent social, cultural, and historical conflict clearly retain a foot in each of the two realms of private self (integrity) and public responsibility (engagement). Being a "good person," in the 21st century as in the 18th, means that each of these often-contradictory demands so condition the other that the whole truly transcends the mere sum of these two parts. My integrity is indebted to my public engagement, and the latter is enriched by my private self.

Keeping such an ideal before us, we can perhaps see what mustn't be sacrificed in human consciousness, even though it will be altered chemically on a regular basis in a society permeated by psychopharmacology. In a human existence shaped by such treatments, we must have an agenda for responsible human consciousness; we must devise a survivor's manual for "the essential values of human life."

The purpose of such an agenda is to help us tell the difference between an essential human sanity and the calm satisfactions available through psychopharmacology. The term "sanity" is, of course, a value-laden word. We need an agenda oriented to human values even to be able to make a diagnostic judgment about sanity. Such agendas may always be subject to the limitations of perspective at any given time, but clarity about the values in our diagnostic, or therapeutic, routines needs our concerted attention.

To begin the task, let's explore a ready catalogue of human experiences contained in common-sense names of emotions.

List One	List Two	List Three
guilt	love	empathic suffering
fear	desire	personal responsibility
anger	satisfaction	obligation to the future
shame	compassion	finding a sacred value

In List One, we have named human passions that are routinely eliminated by psychiatry as a form of "medical" symptom relief. List Two names experiences that are not intentionally eliminated by psychopharmacology, but which are at risk because they depend in some measure on the emotional content of List One, or at least they depend on the coherence of consciousness, or perhaps on the machinery of glandular secretions, that is lost by eliminating List One. List Three tries to name "essential values of human life" that need the elements of Lists One and Two in order to exist.

This is a preliminary effort. Are the items in List Three really essential values of human life? Or, are they merely one person's opinion, or products of an early 21st-century culture that will pass away as surely as did the Renaissance of the 16th century? We can see ways in which Montaigne's virtues have been durable in a way, but will the continuities since the Renaissance continue into a psychopharmacological age, in which we are all liberated from inconvenient and difficult feelings as routinely as penicillin has liberated us from inconvenient and difficult infections? Further historical reflection is required.

EMOTIONAL NARRATIVES

Emotion names, such as those previously mentioned, are too condensed to consider as part of our question. Each name encompasses various experiences, all of which are alike in that we inevitably understand them in narrative form (Sarbin, 1986). To explore emotions as narratives is to open ourselves to the pushes and pulls, the interpersonal and moral content, of human experience. We will focus on depression and anxiety, with the understanding that the definitions of "depression" and "anxiety" in diagnostic language tends to reduce to measurable, or at least countable, signs, but that such signs by-pass the narrative quality of experience that characterizes human beings (Sarbin, 1986; Sarbin and Keen, 1998).

Depression is said to involve a slowed psychophysical activity, difficulty sleeping, poor appetite, chronic fatigue, poor self-assessment, pessimism, thoughts of unworthiness and guilt, of death and suicide, and an inability to experience pleasure and a helplessness to do anything about any of these things.

Anxiety is said to involve physical tension, with elevated heart rate and breathing, nausea, perspiration, a sense of urgency, impatience, pessimism, and a dreading of the future, restlessness, irritability, and difficulty concentrating. Often in cases of both depression and anxiety, there are certain behavioral results of such experiences, such as interpersonal withdrawal in depression and obsessive or phobic superstitions in the case of anxiety.

These lists of countable symptoms are useful in achieving the reliability of diagnosis; one doctor will look for and see the same experience, or "disease," as any other who is properly trained. In contemporary diagnostic practice, the attention to the narratives of depression and anxiety are only implicitly and unofficially acknowledged.

When we think of the validity, rather than the reliability, of diagnosis, it is the narrative themes, not the number of manifest symptoms from each list, that defines depression and anxiety—or, as I will call them from now on, "sadness" and "fear." These more common emotion names present problems, but even more problematic are the layers of connotation that has come to surround depression and anxiety, both of which are central to the medical and disease-centered diagnostic language.

A professional might call me depressed because she or he can appreciate my sadness. This is empathy. It involves understanding what I say and feeling what I feel, more or less, as I say it. Or she or he might do so because I think about death, am losing weight, sleeping poorly, unable to concentrate, and I vacillate between agitation and fatigue. In the second case, instead of empathy, we have diagnosis, as if the objective presence of these signs scientifically verifies my membership in the category of the depressed. In the first case, the empathic process of appreciating my sadness is imprecise, subject to error in prediction, and would not, in current diagnostic practice, justify such a categorization.

Just as we reject depression in favor of sadness, we should be aware that melancholia was rejected in favor of depression. The motive for that earlier rejection may well have been similar to the motive for our current one; the rejected terms had become medicalized, reified, and made to refer to things different from a concrete human experience. We should always seek to recall such experience; it is the basis of all our knowledge.

At stake is not simply which route justifies the categorization; at stake here is whether such a categorization is a good idea. Wiener (1989), among others, has convincingly shown that the diagnostic path is bad science. Here we want to consider sadness and fear, the experiences: what they are, how we know them when we experience them, which can lead us to see how we can help someone else to do so.

In spite of the elaborate intellectual and professional expenditures by psychologists, the procedures and the products of diagnosis are mostly rhetorical. They legitimate current practice, but they add little to our understanding, if we can appreciate experiences such as sadness and fear. Current clinical practice, in its imitation of medicine, reifies—makes into an objective phenomenon—those experiential problems that people bring to therapists. This reification (1) falsifies psychological understanding through its "distanciated" language of diagnosis, and (2) actively misconstrues the character of the phenomenon brought to our attention in the clinical context. In fact, diagnosis runs the risk of insulting the person in front of me by construing her or his subjective life as a medical object. The possibility that a person might be reassured by medicalizing her or his distress also testifies to the extent to which psychological rhetoric has succeeded. Our culture has trained its members that human stresses and distresses can be solved by expert scientific attention and need not be taken seriously in their own terms.

By making a person's experience into a quasi-medical object, current practice by psychologists and psychiatrists begins with an interpersonal event, a conversation. The practice then moves intellectually to a format appropriate for the classification of scientific objects. Our psychological rhetoric has become more and more scientific, partly because science is rhetorically (as well as practically) successful, and this has led us to imitate the medical model. Such medicalized theory affirms the presence of "disease entities" and in so doing detracts from what is native to human experience: feelings such as sadness and fear, their narrative elaborations, and our personal experiential grasp of such experiences.

Empathic contact tends to be ignored in current practice, which is vehement in its affirmation of professional and scientific mastery of such matters. By giving up empathy, however, we are losing much more than pre-scientific sensitivity. In failing to build on the experiential base of empathic contact, clinical psychology and psychiatry become a charade, an imitation, a pretending, and a fraud. Most clinicians actually do both; they play the medical game—increasingly a bureaucratic and funding game—but they also understand their clients as persons understand persons, in terms of how all human beings understand meaning and importance in their and others' experiences—through grasping the narrative content of that experience.

I want to by-pass diagnosis and return to empathy. We must see through depression (the diagnosis) in order to remind us of its latent content: sadness (the experience). Anxiety, assumed to be a measurable quantity, has met the same fate. Its latent content is, perhaps surprisingly, the enormously commonplace experience of fear. It is important that human experiences, of both patients and therapists, be returned from their fruitless romance with objectifying science to their natural home of living out and through our own narratives. Our experiential fabric overlaps those of others to make up the rich psychological matrix of intersubjective experience.

RETURNING TO EMOTIONS

In order to see depression as sadness, we need do little more than recall the experiential base of sadness from which depression has been abstracted, reified, operationalized, measured, and made into a disease. To recognize sadness is to recognize a certain narrative structure and content that expresses it, contains it, and makes it comprehensible to human beings. In contrast, to see the disease, major depressive disorder, is to lose the narrative content of sadness. The narrative content of sadness is loss. What is lost by human beings most saliently are material things. But more precisely, what is lost is my personal relation to, involvement with the thing, the person, the situation—that is, the center of loss is an anticipated future.

Note that a major factor in the dynamics of sadness is loss of hope. The hoped-for future, an anticipated breakthrough, or continuation, or a better, or different, or less routine future can also be lost. It is sad to believe that there will be no surprises— what is will always be. It is sad to know that undeveloped potential will never flourish, that the future that might have been is no longer possible. Experiencing an absence of possibilities in my future is the very center of my being sad.

For clinicians, of course, there is also vicarious sadness, in which I feel someone else's sadness. This is not limited to the clinic; in watching a sad movie, my sadness is not about my own future. We grasp the futures that are lost by others as fully as I experience losing a hoped-for narrative future in my own life. We see here the interpenetration of one experience with another, of your experience with mine, and of the future with the present, and we see sadness in all lives.

The disease depression, by comparison, is a sterile concept; and in the Diagnostic and Statistical Manual of the American Psychiatric Association (DSMD), it becomes even more mundane. Such rhetoric forces us to remind ourselves that depressed people are not sick in a medical way at all. They are struggling with life, and they have become overwhelmed by sadness. Therefore, the "happening" of depression is not a happening at all; it is a "doing." Both Theodore Sarbin and Stephen Pepper spell out the meanings of these terms as the difference between events of nature (happening) and those of human behavior (doing). Depression is a doing; it is human action (Wiener, 1989, makes this abundantly clear). Depression does not appear in the clinic randomly; it appears in the lives of people who are sad and whose way of dealing with sadness is inadequate to the amount of loss they undergo. The degree of loss they have experienced is the amount of forfeited future they have experienced, and the nearness they have come to forfeiting the future all together. This forfeiture can refer to suicide, but people can forfeit the future without suicide; they can withdraw, slow down, give up, and begin accumulating the symptoms, any five of a dozen or so qualify them for the diagnosis of major depressive disorder."

However necessary diagnosis may be in our bureaucratic maze of finance and funding, let's not for a minute believe that these symptoms describe the desperate giving up, in the face of accumulated losses, the assault on a hoped-for future—the sadness—that is the center of what we are pleased to call the disease of depression. Depression is really a bureaucratized notion of sadness, and sadness is, like all emotions, a human activity. As is true of any activity, we must ask about the behavioral symptoms: "What is the person trying to do?" What is the narrative content of enacting the symptoms we have conveniently catalogued in the *Diagnostic and Statistical Manual of Mental Disorders* (American Psychiatric Association, 1994)? Prior to this enactment is loss, the loss of a future that was wanted, counted on in some way, without which the usual meanings in life no longer apply. The enactment is first of all a protest, second, an effort at restoration, and third, an effort at compensation.

All of what we call psychopathology is a protest. What our clients are protesting may be buried beneath years of history, out of which they are exploring a new role of protester or patient. In the case of depression, what is protested is the loss and the unfairness of having to undergo this unremitting sadness. Without blaming our depressed patients, we do have to acknowledge that sometimes the protesting becomes a compensation, or perhaps a retaliation, for the loss. Depressed people can be quite aggressive with their depression, and we want both to sympathize with them and to let them know that their protest is not, in fact, getting them what they really want. It is the job of psychotherapy to work all this out.

Interestingly, pharmacotherapy short-circuits the protest by substituting a chemically induced happiness. If we use pharmacology at all—and it is hard, even foolish perhaps, not to do so—it should never be a substitute for working through the project, the "doing," of protest.

When we must use such a chemical substitute, we should know we are exercising a last resort. It is noteworthy that current practice, by making pharmacotherapy a first resort, enacts much more pessimism than serves many patients well. To indulge our convenience by prescribing drugs, we say to patients that they are unable to see what and why they are protesting. Psychopharmacology runs the risk of insulting our patients.

If people diagnosed with depression are enacting a narrative of protesting their sadness and the life that has saddened them, can we say also that people diagnosed with an anxiety disorder are enacting a narrative of protesting their fear? The fear itself is a narrative; it recounts past events that seemed at the time life threatening. But like sadness, fear anticipates the future. In this case, future assaults. Or, ironically, fear even provokes them.

With anxiety-ridden patients, the threat to their sense of the future is having been surprised by hurt, as opposed to the narrative of past guilt and self-blame of depressed patients. Therefore, the future seems to promise what they remember has frightened them, and that is the occasion, most of all, of present fear, not present sadness. If future repetition is feared in anxiety disorders, then the working out of the fear is working through the protesting of past hurts. It is working within the narrative of one's life.

For both depressed and anxious clients, the future is dreaded. In anxiety, this dread is because the coming hurt is unpredictable. In depression, it is because it is all too predictable. Fear protests but also prepares for unwanted surprises; sadness protests but also prepares for unwanted sameness. The narratives of both fear and sadness are the occasion of experiencing life in a way that leads to behavior we recognize, and even can measure, as anxiety and depression. Diagnosis is not far behind, but that act derails our attention from the narrative. No wonder pharmacotherapy is so common; it not only is more convenient and more reliable than psychotherapy, it completely by-passes the inconvenient task of taking seriously patients' narrative selves and what they say they are trying to do.

To see the narrative content of emotions is to remind ourselves of forgettable but crucial, facts. The so-called diseases of anxiety disorders and depressive disorders are really elaborate patterns of trying to cope with excesses of sadness and fear. If we presume to help such people, we should first of all understand them. To understand the sciences of emotional production in glandular or neurological terms, and then to pretend that such understanding is sufficient for helping people, is to by-pass the task of understanding people.

People certainly have emotions, and they can become excessive. If we want to understand people, we shall have to resort to how people are. The center of who we are is not glandular machines, nor physiological balances. We are coping with life. Our understanding of our own coping is always a narrative, of our lives or of crucial parts of it. To help people, we have to grasp their emotions, and to grasp their emotions, we have to grasp that center, that narrative content.

NARRATIVE AND PRETENDING

Narrative and pretending seem to be awkward bedmates. The narrative I live depends on biographical facts, and only imposters calculatedly falsify them. But my biographical narrative, from which I derive my identity and enact my life as my own, goes far beyond biographical facts into self-concepts, justified and unjustified self-esteem, fantasy distortion of vaguely remembered events, and outright fabrication so long ago that I have forgotten the truth. Nevertheless, my story is who I am in a way more important than the biographical facts. Themes of motivation and morality permeate my story and shape its course and content. What I thought I was doing is as important as what I objectively did, as far as the narrative is concerned.

We come, then, full circle to pretending, and pretending to be depressed. The fundamental facts about pretending are that we do it more than we admit, that we may often not be sure whether we are doing it, and that we nevertheless go ahead with it because we understand its usefulness in terms of the interpersonal situation at hand. Since we cannot, as human beings, ignore how we are seen by an other in any human interaction and since we inevitably have a double consciousness—of what we are doing/saying and what is being seen/heard by an other or others—pretending is not a remarkable human phenomenon. What is remarkable is that it is so little studied, understood, or even mentioned in the psychological literature.

We distinguish people we trust from those we don't; some of our friends are liars and we know it; some of our patients are too. But lying is an event, a single act; pretending is a posture, a way of life, a style, an identity. Common sense always pays attention to this dimension of human behavior; psychology simply does not. It is not clear why, but it makes me wonder about several things.

First of all, it makes me wonder if the legal system, which makes it a point to tell the truth from falsehood in apprehending criminals, might not know something that psychologists ought to know. Second, at stake, of course, is not someone's property that might be stolen or trust that might be exploited for financial profit, but rather the stuff of human relationships, between persons and within persons.

Role-taking and role-playing are both pretending but necessary in the course of every day in every life. What distinguishes phenomena such as pretending to be depressed is that it is role taking and role playing that is self-deceptive as well as deceptive of others, that it is long term and manipulative, that it seeks to gain advantages or treatment otherwise not forthcoming from others, that it offers oneself a line of self-perception that is less judgmental and more permissive than otherwise is available.

I may express love and caring for my children when I don't, at that very moment, feel that way, and it is important to pretend if that is what my child needs or what the situation requires. I have behaved decently when I felt greedy, pretending the former and concealing the latter. We can hardly criticize that bank teller for pretending when he decides not to steal the money, even though it is a daily thought, perhaps an elaborate fantasy, or even a plan.

CHAPTER SEVEN

Notes on Morality and Ontology

IS MORALITY VESTIGIAL?

The inevitable presence of guilt in any discussion of depression yields several tasks. First, we must explore why certain behaviors, like hurting another, make us feel guilty. Beyond that issue we must explore the deeper question of human ontology—the character of human being—to support our answer. These explorations will inevitably bear on any interpretation of depression that sees guilt as germane. Of course, the content of human morality presents considerable theoretical challenge. An interpretation of morality—of concepts of good and of especially evil—will have to justify any envisioned relation between guilt and depression.

Our theorist of choice is Paul Ricoeur, particularly his *Fallible Man: Philosophy of the Will* (1965), which offers us an exploration of good and evil in terms of human ontology. Before exploring these ideas, however, let me point to the provocative opening of Alistair MacIntyre's book, *After Virtue* (1981): "Imagine that the natural sciences were to suffer the effects of a catastrophe. A series of environmental disasters are blamed by the general public on the scientists. Widespread riots occur, laboratories are burnt down, physicists are lynched, books and instruments are destroyed" (1981, 11). Then, this exercise in imagination moves to a Know-Nothing political party that abolishes science in schools and imprisons the remaining scientists. A reaction against this movement tries to revive science, but their own education has been poor. They had only fragments: experiments detached from their theoretical context, only parts of unrelated theories, instruments whose use had become obscure, and fragments of written articles and books, often carefully preserved, but nevertheless torn and charred.

All these pieces came to inspire a set of practices that these courageous people called physics, chemistry, and medicine. Adults argued with each other as if they were practicing science. Children learned by heart surviving portions and recited as incantations some of the theorems of Euclid. Almost nobody realized that what they were doing was not natural science in any proper sense at all.

In such a culture, people would use such expressions as "mass," "specific gravity," and "atomic weight" in often interrelated ways, resembling at times the ways in which such expressions had been used in earlier times, before scientific knowledge had been so largely lost. What proliferated, however, were rival and competing premises for which no further argument could be given.

MacIntyre now comes to his point: In the modern world, the "language of morality is in the same state of grave disorder as the language of natural science in the imaginary world which I described" (11). He sees our current cultural state as morally ungrounded. Indeed, we possess simulacra of morality; we continue to use many of the key expressions. But we have—largely, if not entirely—lost our comprehension, both theoretical and practical, of morality (11–12).

MacIntyre is even more serious than he sounds, for neither philosophy nor history, as they are currently practiced, can liberate us from our lack of a cultural context within which our language of morality is really intelligible. This is a daring and challenging hypothesis. It is somewhat like that of Roberto Mangabeira Unger, who, in *Knowledge and Politics* (1975), describes the hegemony of liberalism as blinding us to its limitations and its alternatives. The political philosophy of the last three centuries leaves us with only certain apparently insuperable inconsistencies, and several potent clues, suggesting that beyond the inconsistencies lie possibilities for an intelligible moral life.

These inconsistencies are such things as our inability to reconcile universalistic rules (the rule of law) with the insurmountable particularity of individual cases, either practically (and justly) or theoretically (and consistently). The clues are such experiences as love, art, and religion—experiences that are nowadays always separate from everyday life. This separateness accentuates their specialness but also relegates them to the status of mere clues, rather than livable solutions, in a culture whose everyday life has centered itself elsewhere.

MacIntyre and Unger are only two of many contemporary thinkers who argue that morality in the modern age has become vestigial.[1] Neither suggests that a simple restoration is possible, nor even desirable, but both claim that modernity has brought certain costs in the coherence of the stories we tell ourselves about who we are. In terms of this book, these costs appear as the problematic nature of our psychological solutions to human, especially moral, problems.

Not only does defining myself as psychiatrically sick embroil me in issues of failure and (in a less explicit but no less inevitable sense) evil, it does so in a way less conducive to real healing than, say, the full complexity of human culture, its rituals (think of the healing promoted by funerals), its moralities (what this chapter deals with), and (recalling chapter 1) its duplicities.

Of course, thinking psychiatrically or psychologically also opens me to the temptation to imitate real depression, a temptation that threatens to pull me down into regions of being that are dark and mysterious. When thinking psychologically, I am especially vulnerable to that danger because I am, as a modern (not pre-modern) man unfamiliar with what used to be called, quite simply, evil.

RICOEUR'S ANTHROPOLOGY

Ricoeur's quest for the evil in human beings does not assume that good and evil are opposites, nor that evil is actually there to be found, unknown only in its location or detail. It begins instead with the simpler datum that human beings feel guilty. Where in a philosophical anthropology can we locate that guilt?

Psychologists have not been afraid of this question: Freud's theory (1959) of the primal horde, or the presence of conditioned emotional reactions (Hull, 1943), might "locate" morality, but not as moral phenomena. These both reduce morality to psychology.[2] Therefore, we must continue to ask: Whence the fallibility, or the fault, in ourselves, which leads us to such elaborate mediations as our theologies, our legal theories and institutions, and the human sciences and their analyses of power, greed, and alienation? Each of these efforts tries to cope with that guilt and fault by mediating between the infinite and the finite in the constitution of human being.

We shall have to clarify what Ricoeur means by the infinite and the finite, and eventually, we will see that much of human life, and certainly psychopathology, can also be understood as attempts at such mediation between the two. Of course, the infinite is not a very rich part of our educational curriculum. It is reduced to merely a mathematical concept. Its human analogue, or experience, is neither culturally vivid nor educationally important. The infinite in my life is the transcendent capability lent me by my second consciousness. I can detect my own biases by self-detachment, I can transcend causality in my own history, and I can imagine states of affairs not actually present, states toward which to strive, against which to measure my current status, and so on. These human capabilities are infinite because they escape the finitude represented by the closed circle of causality that maps our current understanding of nature. Their escape is through consciousness and imagination, which truly transcend this closed circle.[3]

My infinity contrasts with the finite in my life. In everyday life, of course, ultimate matters such as the content of good and evil escape most of our experiences; what remains is a partial (finite) human perspective. We know much about the closedness of my caused character and even my continual failure to achieve those perfections so relentlessly imagined and so powerfully influential in human affairs. But the entire realm of our ideals, which transcend the circles of causalities, and our human sensitivity to moral questions, is not developed in our educational curriculum, nor is its presence in our culture often much more than the physical presence of churches.

As adult human beings, we, in our more complex consciousness, nevertheless, have an ontological doubleness. Limits are real, and we confront them every day. But transcendence is real too. I know I could have been more careful and not caused suffering. That vision of the "good me," whom I failed to enact, is the painful experience of my own evil, for which I feel guilty. Human limits are apparent in light of the possibility that I could be good; transcending those limits—the possibility of goodness—appears only in contrast to a recognition that I often fail to do so. The finitude of limits makes me guilty, and the infinitude of human possibilities for transcending those limits implies that those limits are inherent dimensions of human consciousness. Guilt, my moral failures, and the continuing possibility of moral successes, being good, are key poles in the experience of human beings.

Ricoeur, therefore, introduces what he calls an ethical vision of the world, in which evil and freedom are understood in terms of one another. An ethical vision of the world puts each of us into the center of any exploration of evil, and we can think about this personally. But theory need not be about particular persons. In general, there is always a human capacity to imagine the possibility of avoiding evil and that makes evil recognizable as evil—the result of human choice rather than merely some natural unpleasantness.

For humans, this capacity is always there whether it is taken up or not. When it is taken up, it is done so deliberately. Frequently, but not always, we try to "do the right thing." Evil is, therefore, evil committed, and we know it. Freedom is discovered in the possibility, indeed in the resulting responsibility, to see the evil we do and to try to avoid it in the future. Such a commitment is a universal human possibility; it is to accept "an ethical vision of the world." With an ethical vision of the world, I also accept a theory of human beings in which we must continually mediate between evil and good, between the finite, the caused and provoked temptations, and the infinite, the effort to reach for the right in ourselves.

This mediation constitutes our moral struggles, our conversations and deliberations, within ourselves. Feeling our freedom assumes the responsibility for evil done, which comes to a self-understanding that is "fraught with meaning." It is the experience of guilt, of course. But even more to the point, Ricoeur claims "the avowal of fault is, at the same time, the discovery of freedom" (1965, xxvi). So, we may say that an ethical vision of the world is widely presupposed in everyday life, and it implies many things. Much of life, including much of psychopathology, is our attempt to deal with the lack of fit between the finite—the limitations—in ourselves, on the one hand, and the infinite—the possibilities—in ourselves, on the other. The mediation of the infinite—the openness of human possibility—and the finite—the determinateness of human desire and causality—comes to a head around the experience of freedom and evil, and it leads us to avow our fault and, in so doing, to rediscover our freedom.

This discovery, however, is complex. Every time we face a choice, we also are aware of ourselves as a history, which includes our fault. The avowal of fault is a remembering of a past that can be brought to bear on the future. In avowing fault, we try to do better. Ricoeur states, "In the consciousness of fault the future attempts to encompass the past, self-discovery shows itself as a recovery, and consciousness uncovers in itself a thickness or density which would not be recognized by a reflection attentive only to the forward elan of the project" (xxvii). Our discovery of our freedom, our discovery of the past, and our discovery of our fault all happen at once, and they are all inherent in human experience—in that complex human consciousness of self and world that characterizes everyday life. If we take human consciousness seriously, in its full measure of complexity, Ricoeur is saying that freedom, memory, and guilt imply one another, and he is asserting that they are present in the mere fact of being conscious at all.

Ricoeur's theory is not simple, for human consciousness is not simple. Being conscious is not a matter simply of the light being on instead of off. Human consciousness always remembers, and it anticipates, even in perceiving the present. The past as remembered enriches the future as anticipated with notions of recovery, and remembering inherent in human consciousness inevitably makes consciousness "fraught with meaning." But there is yet more complexity to human consciousness. Such a consciousness of freedom/fault also "is a recourse to the primordial self beyond its acts," a point that simply strengthens and makes more radical "the undivided causality of the self" (xxvii). All this complexity includes, or is based on, the fact that we are, inevitably, conscious of ourselves as particular persons.

Finally, Ricoeur notes that the consciousness of fault also includes an obscure experience of nonbeing. This obscure experience leads Ricoeurr to declare that any act of the self is inevitably moral. It "does not create by itself all alone all the nonbeing which is in the fault [every conscious act] determines [the self] and makes it its own. The [failure] of fault [in human experience] communicates with an essential [failure in human nature] that passes through the actions of the individual self without lessening the gravity of them for consciousness" (xxviii).

Riceour is one of a number of phenomenological analysts who sees, in the careful description of human conscious experience, both an inherent freedom and an inevitable moral sensibility. Ricoeur sees faulty actions—our consciousness of doing less than we should (think of it as the experience of guilt)—as a kind of reverse participation "which must be rediscovered, traversed, and surpassed by a reflection which would break through to what Nabert calls the primary affirmation" (xxviii). In other words, guilt refers not only to the past, but when we think about it, guilt also implicates the future. The avowal of fault becomes, with these elaborations, a primary affirmation of possible future choices. Such choices imply "an ethical vision of the world." In other words, in the face of guilt, we are led to a reflection on the fault of ourselves. Ricoeur, therefore, concludes that human freedom, human morality, and human fault are all inherent in human experience. "In an ethical vision, not only is it true that freedom is the ground of evil, but the avowal of evil is also the condition for the consciousness of freedom" (xxviii).

If the avowal of evil is the condition for the consciousness of freedom, then there must be some way that the refusal to avow evil, or the denial of evil, undermines our consciousness of freedom. For my blue jay, who is conscious but not self-conscious enough to see the limitations of his own consciousness, there is no consciousness of the possibility to transcend these limitations. Jay consciousness, unlike human consciousness, experiences a sense of the future not informed by a sense of evil committed, whose sense of freedom, and whose self as author, are not understood. The jay's glimpse of nonbeing can be no more significant than mere pain. For such animals, the lack of an avowal of evil is not a denial; it is a lack of the option to avow or to deny.

Human beings, in contrast, have before them the possibility of an ethical vision of the world, and hence, we must either avow it or deny it. Full avowal takes guilt into oneself, which allows human beings to experience possibilities closed to the blue jay—the experience of freedom. Thus, human beings must mediate the ethical aspects of the simultaneous presence, in themselves, of alternatives that are moral. We experience possibility, instead of mere happening; we distinguish possibility from necessity, infinitude from finitude.

As human beings, we experience all sorts of less than full avowals, and whatever else is true of psychopathologies, it is true of them that they are also always experienced in some way different from a simple version of an ethical interpretation of the world. Of course, even in psychopathology, an outright denial of human freedom is rare as a personally lived ideology. Some abnormal states do exaggerate, or even embrace, sin and evil, or suffer from their centrality.

But side by side with this, and more typically, freedom is affirmed and my committed evil is denied, projected, or rationalized. We know from such historical events as Nazi Germany that such a posture is also not rare in "normal" human experience. It can become a part of society and be officially sanctioned by the moral authorities of society. Some theorists refer to this posture as "pride."[4]

Ricoeur's analysis of the locus of human fallibility is not much different than a theory of pride, although it remains more general. His efforts eventually focus on the *Gemut* (feeling) of respect for persons and its possible perversion. This *Gemut* mediates the finitude (the givenness) of one's character and the infinitude (openness, possibility) of *eudaemonia* (the Greek ideal of the good and happy life).

This feeling of respect for persons combines the narrowness of one's openness to the world (the finitude of character) with the ideal of the good life (infinitude of human freedom) by making possible the notion of a person, or the essence of personhood, toward which we personally strive.

How does human consciousness, and particularly our experience of other people, combine the finitude of character and the infinitude of human freedom? Ricoeur observes that a feeling of respect for human beings "designates a thing quality [we see the girl as a lovable object] and, through this thing quality, manifests, expresses, and reveals the inwardness of I" (128–129). Feelings for people are thus paradoxical; they place persons as both subject and object. Like knowing, feelings are part of our intentional relation to the world, but unlike knowing, which objectifies and creates distance between the subject and the object, feelings tie me more intimately to the world. "Our 'affections' are read into the world they develop, which reflects their kinds and nuances" (127). Without feelings, the world is distant and alien; through feelings it becomes interiorized. In this sense, the blue jay of chapter 1 has feelings, but it has none of the character of human feelings that enrich what otherwise can be detachment, manipulation, calculation, and indifference.

Human fallibility, then, lies in the fragility of affects and their liability to be changeable. This liability can be traced to the duality of ends human beings must always bridge. On the one hand, we seek the perfect good life—*eudaemonia*, happiness. On the other hand, pleasure is what we want, also perfect in its presence but, alas, temporary and for that reason finite. We want pleasure but not its finitude. This wanting bespeaks an infinite pole toward which pleasure wants to be drawn and with which it wants to be synthesized. Tragically, human beings are apt to see the objects of pleasure, with their objectivity and stability, as the solution to the temporariness of pleasure. The real case, however, is that pleasure and happiness are part of a larger relation of disproportion, a lack of fit, a noncoincidence of humans with themselves, which is the original "fault" of fallibility.

Happiness (*eudaemonia*) implies reason; pleasure does not. Reason criticizes the closedness of pleasure and opens it, through constraint, to a higher form. But this mediation is never complete; reason takes much of human experience into account beyond the biological patterns of pleasure. It takes one's situation, the culture at large, its norms and ideals all into account. There is no single formula. Happiness is not a state; it is a goal toward which all action ultimately aims, grasped by our powers of reason but only simulated in the concrete experience of pleasure, even though this experience is expanded and consolidated through the objects of pleasure supplied by the culture.

Pleasure is not evil, nor is having, or power, or feeling self-worth, although their perverted forms of greed, tyranny, and vainglory are common topics in the analysis of sin. It is only the perversion of having, power, and self-worth that are evil, and this perversion emerges in our struggles with disproportionality, between the finite and infinite, between character and happiness, and between pleasure and *eudaemonia*. These are all part of the lack of coincidence of humans with themselves, where feelings are led, and in turn lead us astray. Less capriciously, respect for others combines the "humanity" of *eudaemonia* with the finitude of character and pleasure, but it is a fragile *Gemut*, easily lost in the crosscurrents of passion. Ricoeur recalls Aristotle's description of *humos* and its ambiguous fate.

This account of Ricoeur's philosophical anthropology offers us a ground for our analysis. The denial of evil committed, the indulgence in pride, somehow results in the loss of well-being we call depression. I have suggested that if the avowal of evil committed is the condition of the experience of freedom, then that experience is somehow undermined by our denial, projection, or rationalization of evil committed. These all serve pride and corrupt the mediation of our finitude with our infinitude, our primordial guilt with an ethical vision of the world. The inevitability of our guilt is part of our finitude. This guilt generates the symbols so striking in the history of human self-consciousness, and these symbols attempt the mediation of the guilt with the ethical demand for goodness.

According to Ricoeur, behind this version of finitude and infinitude lies an even deeper "opposition" of which man is a "fragile synthesis": "the opposition of originating affirmation and of existential difference." The opposition finds its voice in the non-necessity that I exist, a realization whose terminus is "a negative lying deeper than all the language, and which we may epitomize, following Spinoza, in the excellent word, 'sadness'" (214). Thus, we see the human situation as "the becoming of an opposition" (216), "the 'mixture' of originating affirmation and existential negation. Man is the Joy of Yes, available in our ability to see the possibility for good. But we always see it in the sadness of the finite" (215), our having failed to be as good as we could be.

DEPRESSION AND SADNESS

The sadness of the finite is not depression. It is more like guilt. Sadness surrounds and configures my life, but my sadness is shaped by the joy of affirmation. Guilt is also the call of possibility. Not all finitude, not even the most profound negativity in the core of my being, makes me depressed. If guilt makes me sad, in turn it is the occasion of remembering my originating affirmation. Sadness saddens but does not swallow me up and preclude another day, another time, another moment of life. Sadness can be mediated. It can be absorbed into my future plans that recognize that about which I am sad. It can be taken into my self and synthesized into a life that survives sadness and lives its affirmations. This sort of achievement is possible generally in dealing with the finite. People can be, and often are, good.

Even the partiality of my perspective can be synthesized with the objectifying power of speech to produce a widened perspective. The closedness of character can be combined with the possibility of essential humanity in *eudaemonia* to produce respect for persons. The guilt of evil committed can be synthesized with my open future and, with my effort to be good, can produce a sense of my own freedom. Of course, there can also be failures. The finite can also fail to be synthesized. It can be ignored or denied, lost to pride. Without sadness there are no affirmations; without my partiality of perspective there is no perception, but only clichés and general truth claims. Without the closedness of my character, there is no respect for persons who see things differently, but only empty formulae of universal love for others. Without the guilt of evil committed, there is only the illusion of goodness, that is pride, enslavement to that which undermines my sense of my freedom.

It is this last, pride and an undermining of my sense of freedom, that we must now explore further, to investigate not the symbols of evil that Ricoeur pursues but a different kind of phenomenon: clinical depression. How exactly does pride lead to depression? Pride is the denial, projection, or rationalization of evil committed; it is the failure to deal with this particular aspect of my finitude, a failure to bring to bear on it the healing synthesis of the avowal of guilt. Avowal synthesizes guilt with an ethical demand; pride refuses this avowal, avoids this synthesis; it leaves guilt unsynthesized to poison our ethical efforts. This poisoning undermines the concrete grounds for my sense of self-worth, a widely recognized issue in depression (Bibring, 1953). Self-worth requires from me, in order to be concrete, actions taken toward a future whose meaning is informed by the past, including evil committed. I am worthy, in my own estimation, if (and only if) I move into the future as a part of a historical process—a historical process in which good and evil actively conflict, and my action matters.[5]

The evils of human history either have something to do with me or they do not. Pride affirms the latter. It puts the starving children, the tortured political prisoners, the liquidated Jews and murdered Indian tribes on another planet, in a different world, apart from me. I live on an island of safety and sanity whose purity must be protected lest the insanity of human suffering stain my life. My self-worth depends on these evils having nothing to do with me.

What is depression after all? It is sadness, but sadness without a future, sadness run wild, sadness unmitigated by the redeeming elements of life. Under what conditions does sadness, which is finally grounded in human finitude, envelop my life with the oppressiveness of depression? How is sadness mitigated? What are the redeeming elements of life that enable me to survive sadness? The psychology of self-worth is enormously complex. The concrete actions that underlie self-worth, the capability of pride's entry, disguised as self-worth, the possibilities and impossibilities of my concretely affecting the course of human history all need to be brought into account.

Finitude must include not only my guilt for evil committed but also my impotence to affect concretely the human suffering so apparent at every turn. It is strenuous to mediate this finitude with the demands of an ethical vision of the world through concrete action. Such action moves into a future informed by evil committed in the past, and it depends on feelings, such as my *Gemut* for persons, my respect. Finally, such actions must deal with the human fault, the disproportionality, one's lack of coincidence with oneself, which in turn creates a maelstrom of feelings in which pride inserts itself.

Pride deceives me about my self-worth in the same way pleasure deceives me about happiness. Pleasure is substantive while happiness (*eudaemonia*) is adjectival, the "how" of something else. Yet happiness is that toward which all action aims. However, the aiming of this action is not substantive; it is not a state. It is, rather, an adjective of my life. By aiming at the mere state, I close off what is necessary for my life to be happy. A state is finite and temporary; its pursuit is endless and restless. In itself, it fails, exhausted. *Eudaemonia* is not a state as much as it is a way of being that synthesizes the finitude of pleasure with the infinitude of reason. This synthesis opens the closed limits of pleasure, through critique and through constraint, to a higher level. The failure of this synthesis is the fate of all of us occasionally and a few of us totally. It is our guilt; it reflects our fallibility.

Pride is substantive: "I am a good person." Self-worth is adjectival: "What I am doing is a good thing to do." Yet goodness is the demand of an ethical vision of the world. That demand, however, is not for the goodness of myself but for the goodness of my actions. It is for an adjectival, rather than a substantive goodness, a "how" of my actions, not a pure state of my self. By aiming at the state, I close off what is necessary for my actions to be good. The state, the goodness of my self, is temporary. To pursue it, as to pursue pleasure, is endless and restless and, finally, hopeless.

This guilt, so necessary for my primary affirmation and my freedom nevertheless sometimes overwhelms me, consumes me, defeats me, envelops me. Like sadness run wild, guilt run wild can be unmitigated by the redeeming elements of life. In both cases, the finitude of human being loses hope, remains as an unsynthesized poison that undermines my future, its capability for actions that are good, and therefore my self-worth.

We may, then, finally, say that depression is a distinct human possibility. It is grounded in human finitude. But humans also partake of infinitude. The synthesis of finitude and infinitude is Ricoeur's way of describing the struggles of life, a task that is, finally, destined to a universe of complications. These complications inevitably concern, as Aristotle saw, human feelings, their possibilities for synthesizing such incommensurables as the closedness of my character and the universality of essential humanity, but also their propensity to lead us astray, to deceive us, indeed to trap us into patterns of being that flail around, collapsing in exhaustion.

Our susceptibility to depression is surely affected by what happens to us; we suffer losses early in life and never cease needing to compensate for them, and we suffer blows later in life and frantically try to sustain a self whose identity has been assaulted. The relation of such external causes to depression—later causes that assault us directly and the earlier ones that shape our characters—is not a mechanical one. We translate these causes and effects into our decisions about how to deal with the demands of an ethical vision of the world and with the inevitability of finitude. Our sadness, our guilt, our self-doubts are inevitable. Depression is not.

However, depression understood without these demands is depression misunderstood. Surely a human ontology or a philosophical anthropology by itself is an incomplete explanation of depression, for every concrete case is a case of a particular history. But no accounting for a particular history can take place without an anthropology. Ricoeur's description of human struggles not only supplies such an anthropology but also enlightens us about what has to be taken into account.

SOME CONCLUSIONS

It is now necessary to return to our earlier discussion of depressive narratives and kinds of depression. Recall that I distinguished pretending to be depressed, or pseudodepression, from the giving up of real depression. Both of these are different from agitated depression, which is depressive, but still struggling and hence is not only depressive.

If pride, the denial of one's evil committed, is made up of the stuff Ricoeur envisions in the ontological structure of human being, it can then be said to lead, by a complicated but not incomprehensible route, to human depression. This is one route to depression. But there are also the phenomena of personal narratives biased on the side of culpability and how these make one vulnerable to the magnetic vortex of real depression. Surely those guilt-biased narratives, which we called without hesitation "depressive narratives" are really depressive and that suggests a second route to depression, in a way that is opposite of pride.

There is yet a third route to depression. Individuals who play with giving up may become genuinely depressive; they may get sucked into the temptations and fascinations of peace instead of struggle, even a sort of living death. Until this happens, such individuals enact all sorts of interpersonal patterns that play with giving up. They are pretending; they are, fortunately and life-savingly, duplicitous. However, unsupported by a culture that encourages Ricoeur's synthesizing, oblivious to an ethical vision of the world, this duplicity is unstable and unreliable as a protection against real depression.

I believe all three of the routes to depression—pride, depressive narratives, and pseudodepression—are very old. They appeared in earlier times. But they are given a certain twist in the modern age, where "the ethical vision of the world" at once is a universal possibility, thrust into our lives by the global consciousness of the modern world. An ethical vision of the world is also supported by the structure of our double consciousness, and yet ethical and moral thought has increasingly become isolated from other centers of life, other themes, preoccupations, cultural ideals that characterize modernity. Is "vestigial" too strong a word to describe the fading of morality from the center of life in modern times?

It is possible to speculate that the cost of such fading, in the face of the continuing vivid presence of, say, human suffering—and, therefore, of the possibility of an ethical vision of the world—leaves us even more severely out of joint with ourselves than otherwise we would be. We must, in modern times, mediate not only between the finitude and infinitude in ourselves, but also between the traditional mediations (such as morality, religion, myth) and our contemporary culture that is increasingly indifferent to human suffering.

A parallel complexity engulfs our dealing with sadness, loss, and other such inevitable difficulties in life. We mediate sadness through a future, part of which is our ethical commitment. As that mediation receives less and less support from the culture at large, sadness looms up unmediated, yielding hopelessness, helplessness, and meaninglessness. Our substitute attempt to mediate life through psychological concepts of illness proves particularly maladjusted. Psychiatry offers me the right to be a patient, but it cannot engage me in the same mobilizing of resources to meet the challenge as can the demand of an ethical vision of the world. It lacks the grandeur, the stature, the inspiration to move us. It is, finally, petty and inadequate to the demands of life.

CHAPTER EIGHT

Guilt and Depression

KINDS OF GUILT

Essential Guilt

Essential guilt is guilt for what or who I am, rather than guilt for what I have done. Both are part of our mental life. While Ricoeur has convinced us that guilt can become part of a more sensitive future, expiation is strenuous. Taking this seriously, this chapter will seek to elaborate Ricoeur's insight, beginning with a distinction between guilt that is inherent, or "essential," and guilt that we can call "existential."

Essential guilt predates all its content. I may feel guilt for being white in a society whose ancestors enslaved blacks or whose soldiers slaughtered Vietnamese. I may feel guilt for having torn my mother's flesh at birth, for being a descendant of Adam and Eve, or for forcing my parents to give up things they wanted in order to feed and clothe me as a child. Each of these contents makes me culpable for something I didn't do, in the usual sense of doing something. Each can also become blatantly irrational and neurotic. But the irrationality or neuroticism is not the origin of the guilt. This guilt is already there, inherent in our being. It makes us ready to be irrational and neurotic in these ways, but it also underlies our capacity for humility, forgiveness, and respect. Its content may change; its presence, while not always manifest, is constant.

This guilt is a human limit. In terms of essential guilt, I cannot be "not guilty," no matter how hard I try. In the face of essential guilt, I am indeed hopeless and helpless to overcome it. Essential guilt lies right at the edge of my identity. Its common border with my identity creates a profile so that who I am is defined by essential guilt, and I can ignore this border only in distraction, in active escape from what I really know—that I owe the contour of who I am to that guilt, which predates my current identity and surrounds me on every side. Any time I am not pulled up into the center of myself, in pride or arrogance, I am apt to be drawn over the edge, beyond my everyday self, into the depths of who I am beside this innocent identity I so casually but desperately boast. That larger being of who I am, into which I was born, is essentially guilty.

Experiencing essential guilt can lead me to give up, as in pure depression, or it can enter into my narrative, my identity, in such a way as to provoke humility, forgiveness, and respect. My narrative—and identity—either absorb and accommodate such guilt, or they deny it. The denial falsifies my narrative and makes it vulnerable to collapse. If the collapse is anxious, I may resort to pseudodepression or agitated depression, and their narrative possibilities. If it is not, then I must live my essential guilt. The narratives of essential guilt appear in most religions, but not only there. An awareness of essence, preceding time and even a world within which to strive to be good, allows no possible outlet from the *cul de sac* of essential guilt. The meanings, for a human life, that are possible derivatives of essential guilt are in our modern period increasingly thin versions of religiosity that encourage me to feel good, saved, or obedient.

Essential guilt in the last century or so fits badly with the commercial pleasures and secular pride of modernity, so that considerable anxiety and struggle are necessary not to surrender into triviality. The risk of the struggle is to be pulled into the various temptations to give up.

Pretending to be depressed, feeling unexplainable guilt or sadness, struggling with giving up, and all the other versions of what we call "depression," combine with scientific aspects of our culture to create specters of psychiatric categories. The essential guilt that underlies all this can be embraced and lived existentially, where we do things, for moral reasons, and care about how to live. But essential guilt can also engulf our entire narrative and leave all purpose for struggle in a collapsed state of exhaustion.

Existential Guilt

We do, therefore, struggle. In agitated depression, I seek to retain a story, to transform the inner opacity of essential guilt into a more familiar, more palpable and livable guilt—guilt for having done something. The agitated quest—for what I did to be so guilty—or the agitated conclusion—that I killed my father, or I spat in the face of God—are struggles that seek to transform the guilt into existential guilt.

In contrast to essential guilt, existential guilt stems from what I did. Atonement for sins and expiation and amends for damages done to others, while never simple, have the flavor of possibility instead of impossibility. To construe my life as guilty in this fashion is to build a narrative that has a future, some point toward which to aim, when the injured party will be compensated, the wrong righted, and the uncanny stickiness of guilt alleviated.

Existential guilt also is a human limit insofar as we seek to be guiltless. For we never escape violating a trust, neglecting an obligation, or hurting another no matter how hard we try. But it is a constantly shifting limit, one that changes as our lives proceed through the violations and expiations that make up our usual days and weeks. The narrative possibilities of existential guilt not only have a future of righting the wrong, or becoming part of "a more fully synthesized" and thus expiated guilt. Such narrative possibilities also do not get sucked up into the totalism of essential guilt. I am always more than guilty while I am striving to make amends. In contrast, my essential guilt, in the face of the collapse of my narrative, can grow to consume me. Existential guilt cannot. Struggles of "I shouldn't" and "I won't," not in themselves depressive, become depressive exactly when they involve essential guilt. The "I shouldn't" becomes the "I shouldn't have" of commission and the "I won't" becomes the "I willed it not" of omission.

These references to the past create a future obligation to make it right, but they also create guilt, which is already there as a potential and an essence of my being. Guilt for having done (or not done) something is not essential guilt, but it gravitates toward it nonetheless, confronting me with what and who I am as well as what I've done, pulling me into the abyss against which I must desperately struggle if I am to have a story, a future, a meaning at all. Existential guilt cannot consume me, but it can pull me into the orbit of essential guilt, which eventually can.

Angry Guilt

I feel guilty not only for my past but for my present feelings, most notably for my anger. I may be so angry that I am dangerous, and I may protect others from that danger by entering into the equally impressive danger of turning the anger back against myself. The frenzies of self-punishment seen in agitated depression are also the paradigmatic Freudian melancholia. Convincing as Freud's descriptions and interpretations are, I have said that the resulting guilt, the anger directed back at myself, is not really guilt. It is neither essential guilt nor existential guilt, although it may masquerade as either. The Freudian guilt is thus a pretense. The affect is not really guilt but anger, and the object is not really myself but another.

Freud did not, and psychoanalysts generally do not, understand guilt as either essential or existential, but as derivative from an ontology of instincts and energy distribution. All guilt thus appears to be merely anger turned back on myself. I obviously disagree with that interpretation of guilt, but I do not disagree that anger can be turned dangerously back on myself. Sometimes I experience that anger as anxiety and sometimes I experience it as guilt. If such an anger is experienced as guilt, it is a pretense, not real guilt. Self-degradation and endless self-criticism betray their pretense in that they can never be relieved by proof of self-worth. If they can be relieved by leading my future behavior toward some kind of goodness, then that self-directed anger is more like existential guilt. But the experience of self-punishment and self-degradation, even if it is pretentious turning anger back on myself, can, like existential guilt, be pulled into the orbit of essential guilt, calling into the fray the presence and power of essential guilt.

Thus, essential guilt, as an experience, either enters and is avowed by my ongoing narrative, curbing my pride, or it is denied, falsifying my narrative and my identity. The falsification increases my vulnerability to the collapse of my narrative and, thus, to being swallowed up by essential guilt. With or without struggle, this collapse can lead to giving up. Spurred on by anger, suicide becomes a choice way to express that giving up. Angry guilt can become pathological guilt, not genuine guilt. It is anger, now pretentious, but not, for that reason, less dangerous.

Pretending Guilt

We return, finally, to pseudodepression, that much more cheerful condition of being anxious and merely pretending to be depressed. We know well enough how we pretend to feel guilty, thereby augmenting our request for love and acceptance, now in the form of forgiveness. I am anxious that my pretense may be discovered, that my guilt will be exposed, that my assumed narrative of the guilty one will lose its ability to make my life meaningful, and my story will collapse. As before, my pretentious guilt can be pulled into the orbit of essential guilt and, like existential and angry guilt, can eventuate in something much more serious.

It is amazing how often my pretending to be depressed does engage me in struggles with both essential and existential guilt. These struggles can become truly depressing because my pretensions engage me in both doing and being evil. Therapy for pseudodepression, therefore, must both be different from and like therapy for agitated and pure depression.

GUILT, EVIL, AND DEPRESSION

The core of depression lies in our essential guilt. Human beings possess a double consciousness, which condemns them to the internal rift between the good we could possibly be and the less-than-good we actually are. As a species, human beings are, in their make-up, guilty. This is not a feeling, created by culture or parents. It is an aspect of the human situation and the human essence, whether we feel it or not, which nearly all of us do so vividly, and whether culture and parents bring it into focus or not—and, of course, nearly all parents do exactly that.

We are guilty because we are evil. Now, much has been made of human evil, sometimes as if it were a great surprise as to how essentially benevolent characters like human beings could do such things, or sometimes as if it were no surprise at all in light of God's perfection and our continual failure to live up to that standard. There have also been indignant rebellions against theories of human evil, as if such a notion is merely superstitious and, in the light of reason, can be exposed as dispensable dogma.

I am sometimes puzzled by all this controversy. We live in a society that does many good things, but we also exploit the resources and the people of less developed countries; we sell arms and even nuclear know-how for profit around the world; we challenge others to match our arms production; we spend hundreds of thousands of dollars on a single war plane and tens of thousands of dollars on school lunches. Looking back in history, the Vietnam War, Nazism, the Spanish Civil War, World War I, American slavery, the genocide of American Indians all provide little doubt about human evil. Of course, our nation is not alone. Virtually every people has such a history. Whence the doubt about human guilt? I did not personally kill any Indians or Vietnamese, but am I really pure where my predecessors were tainted? I certainly have supported, with my taxes, a government that invades foreign lands and sells nuclear missiles around the world, even during disarmament negotiations. It is easy enough to be a complicitor in contemporary evil.

Even if all this were not persuasive, I would have to answer for the personal pain I cause others—my family, my friends, my students. I am no more malicious than the next fellow, of course, but I regularly forget obligations, neglect others' sufferings, and even add to it inadver-tently—or sometimes consciously, reckoning that their suffering is less important than my convenience. We all do these things. It's easy and as inevitable as taxes. Every institution I participate in conveys my being into the realm of public action, some of which is racist, profiteering from a stock market that supports industries that exploit the poor, and so on. If we who make up such institutions are not responsible for that evil, then who is?

So human beings are evil; part of who and what I am is evil. What part? In what sense is some part evil? Are there other parts that are not evil? It almost sounds as though evil is in us only in the sense that evil is in the tiger who kills and eats the lamb. What is in the tiger is hunger and a stalking, pouncing, and eating instinct. What is not in the tiger is the possibility of an ethical view of the world.

Also not in the tiger is a consciousness of how it must feel to be a lamb who is stalked, pounced, and eaten, nor even the possibility of such a consciousness, nor a consciousness that there are alternatives to stalking, pouncing, and eating lambs, nor an after-the-fact capability to put this empathy together with an awareness of alternatives and to plan to eat next time, causing less pain for others.

Such plans, not about eating, perhaps, but about most of what we do, are nearly inevitable in human beings. So is the notion of "better" and "worse" plans, of "good" and "evil." No human being yet known, except perhaps for the few feral children who have been found, is free of consciousness of good and evil. Consciousness of good and evil is a consciousness of morally different alternatives; it is a moral conscious-ness. Our moral consciousness is in us, in a way, but not like shoes that are in a box. Rather, we are moral creatures; our being is moral. In this way, morality and evil is part of human nature. It is inherent in being human. The morality, the evil, and the guilt are ontologically given.

The upshot of this line of thought is not that we should wallow in our guilt, writhing in self-condemnation; it also does not necessarily follow that we should seek redemption for our sins through any particular religious agency. An awareness of human guilt, and my personal guilt, does, however, preclude the arrogance and pride integral to much of modern capitalism, humanism, and liberalism. To err, then, is human; to be human is to err, to be guilty, to do evil along with whatever good we also no doubt do. Pretending that this is not so, being proud of my freedom from evil, is a falsification of who I am. This is an ontological falsification and it has far-reaching consequences for my psychic life. Finally, it leads to a vulnerability to depression.

I believe it was Karen Horney (1950) who made clear to me the connection between pride and guilt. The pride of guiltlessness is inherently unstable, for every waking minute threatens to present me with data attesting to my guilt. It is an anxious task to sustain my pride of guiltlessness, and yet I do it when I scratch my head in puzzlement over the inhumane treatment of political prisoners in Latin America, or when I am surprised that an enlightened person like myself could get so angry and say such hurtful things. Indeed, if my concept of myself is guiltless, I will be threatened by such a realization. I will deny or rationalize or project my guilt, leading to further insensitivity and more elaborate evil, which in turn will have to be denied, rationalized, or projected.

My psychological situation is really more complex than this, however. It is not merely a self-concept that is at stake. A self-concept is a part of the larger and more permanent narrative, which expands in at least two directions, temporally into a history and a future, and socially into a group identity, which also has a history and a future. That group story is also my personal story insofar as I am (my being is) a part of the group.

When my narrative, the context of meaning within which I find myself intelligible, collapses, I find myself unintelligible. What was 1945 like for the convinced Nazi or the loyal Japanese whose entire lives had become manifestations of a narrative that suddenly collapsed? Were there not many Americans whose loyal Americanism suffered a collapse with the Vietnam War, or with Watergate, impeachments, stolen elections, and other such national disgraces? The collapse of such group narratives never completely disorients a person unless there remains no personal narrative that transcended the group identity.

But personal narratives are no less subject to collapse. The German *Hausfrau* who had two main narratives in terms of which her life was intelligible, the Nazi myth and her family, suffered a double collapse if her national narrative and her familial narrative were simultaneously destroyed by the demise of her nation and the deaths of her husband and sons. Death of a loved one, in any case, always brings a collapse of part of our personal narrative, that intelligibility upon which we depend even in order to get out of the bed in the morning.

The more a loss surprises me, the more unprepared I am for it, the more devastating is its effect on me. I periodically prepare myself for losses by imagining them and imagining myself going on. Such ruminations are far from idle; they rehearse a continuation of a personal narrative; they establish its viability and plausibility independent of dispensable others. They inoculate me against the traumas of loss, lessening their shock and situating them within a larger story that can encompass them and make them intelligible without life becoming empty.

Just as a consciousness of the possibility of loss inoculates me against its traumatic impact, so does the consciousness of my evil inoculate me against the impact of the discovery of my guilt. Yet, this analogy is not the whole story. The presence of guilt is more powerful than the inevitability of loss, for guilt, that essential guilt that is inevitable and a part of my very being, can never be overcome. I cannot recover from it, as I can a loss. I can make amends for the things that I do, but I cannot overcome the guilt that has to do with who I am, which in turn has to do with the evil that I did not personally participate in, such as this or that war crime, but evil that is as much in me as it is in those who did.

My guilt then is more pervasive and more powerful; it lurks at the edge of my self-concept and my narrative and threatens to infiltrate it, implicating me in those atrocities I ordinarily reserve for the bad people of the world. Every trauma that threatens the integrity and coherence of my narrative simultaneously threatens that aspect of my story that denies and flees from essential guilt. I, therefore, blame myself for the loss of a relationship, even if it is not my fault. I even feel guilty in the face of a death of a loved one—an irrational feeling, of course, but not the feeling of a deranged mind. It is, simply, my inability to handle my essential guilt successfully in the face of a loss.

Essential guilt cannot be atoned. Existential guilt can. Essential guilt is for what I am, while existential guilt is for what I do. As I pick my way through the markets of life, experiencing options, taking some, rejecting others, doing good things and doing bad things, I find that the expiation of my guilt makes a meaningful sequence. I do something wrong, feel guilty, and then I try (as Ricoeur notes) to make up for my shortcoming, and then feel better. This constantly revolving sense of guilt and expiation is an important part of my narrative. It keeps my narrative oriented toward a future, where I will be better, I will make up for evil I've done, I will have a relatively clear conscience. This is the cycle of existential guilt, for what I've done, and it is an important part of my and everyone's life.

Essential guilt, in contrast, does not yield to expiation. If I am a traditional Christian, I might, through faith in the grace of God, have hope of relief from this guilt. But that is the only way I can do so, and certainly such a faith is no cure-all for essential guilt. It promises, but it also demands; a covenant is a two-edged sword. Essential guilt haunts me. I may be quite irrational in my attempt to make it intelligible to myself, such as blaming myself for the inconvenience I caused my parents by being born. But such irrationality is not a sign that the guilt is pathological. The guilt is normal. My attempt to explain, to master it through saying why I feel guilty, may be pathological, but the guilt behind it is already there.

Now, I have said that I am intelligible to myself because I place myself in a narrative, a story of my life and of my reference group, that has a past and a future. As Ricoeur notes, the future is especially important. It is the future toward which I aim in doing anything I do, except perhaps for those moments of pure consummation. Depression occurs when my future promises nothing new—no growth, no movement—but rather only a repetition of the past, the same thing again, with no relief, no escape, no change; my narrative leads nowhere and the passage of time ceases to matter. In an important way, such a state of affairs defines depression. I give up. Ricoeur's possibility of synthesis disappears. I no longer strive for anything. That state of having given up is the purest form of depression.

Essential guilt, as I have described it, offers nothing to our narrative possibilities. It is essential, not subject to change. No atonement possibilities make the future different from the present and the past. Essential guilt, then, undermines the future in my narrative; it thus undermines my narrative's capacity to make my life intelligible. Essential guilt, unlike existential guilt, gives me no reason to get out of bed in the morning.

This subversive nature of essential guilt means that it can, and sometimes does, totally engulf an individual. It can so thoroughly undermine one's narrative that life becomes empty, meaningless, unintelligible. Essential guilt can be a spiritual cancer; it can grow and destroy those aspects of our psychic lives that make life tolerable, our meaning-giving narratives with their future possibilities toward which we strive.

But essential guilt does not always do this to me. When it does not, why not? Why am I not depressed all the time? How do I keep my narrative intact in the face of essential guilt? Here again, the analogy of loss may help—how the rehearsal of the possibility of loss can make plausible to me a continuing saga of myself without the lost other. The corresponding inoculation against essential guilt is humility—an understanding of evil, in myself and in others, that enables me to forgive others and have respect for them, even in their (and my) most evil moments.

As Horney (1950) made clear, pride and guilt go together; they are not opposites, but rather they imply one another. The opposite of pride is humility, which does not make me guiltless but enables me to absorb, live with, and survive my guilt rather than be overwhelmed by it. Humility is also, therefore, the antidote to depression—that giving up in the face of overwhelming essential guilt. Indeed, no striving may relieve me of my essential guilt, but it can relieve my existential guilt, at least temporarily. Striving can also lead to many other things that are good and worthwhile, not pure, not guiltless, not Godlike—ideals of perfection in the face of which we always fail—but nevertheless better than other things. To see one future possibility as better than another, even though it is not absolutely good, is to see the importance of my striving for it. As long as I am able to do this hopefully, vigorously, and yet humbly, I cannot be depressed.

THERAPY AND DUPLICITY

Therapy for pseudodepression must deal with losses and their implications, namely the rigor of reinventing myself for the future, and the rigor of reaffirming myself and my past. Reinventing myself must face the openness of the future and its accompanying anxiety. Reaffirming myself must face my boundedness to the past, including my losses and its accompanying sadness. Both tasks are postponed by pretending, including, especially, pretending to be depressed.

These therapeutic goals can be restated in terms of meaning, that is, in terms of narrative. I must forego the story of myself I have borrowed and return to my own story. To engage my own story, I have to incorporate the following seven features of narrative, each of which is rigorous; and, in each case, giving in to pretending is a tempting alternative:

1. I have to *continue*, that is, to remain related to origins, to acknowledge and embody a debt to my origins and an obligation to perpetuate something.

2. I have to continue an *enactment*, which means that action is called for the creation of visible, irreversible, objective and public behavior.

3. I have to continue an enactment of a *narrative*, which means that the coherence of a story constrains me from being someone whose action is incoherent.

4. I have to continue an enactment of a narrative, some of which is given, such as the particulars of my *Geworfenheit*, my family, my century, my race, nationality, and gender.

5. Some of my narrative must be created by me, which means that I am responsible for how the story finally comes out. Its shape, while surely constrained by circumstances, is vividly up to me.

6. I have to continue an enactment of a narrative that I understand, which makes it invalid to pretend not to understand it. Of course, my understanding at any given time is subject to grow, become more complete and vivid.

7. Others understand my narrative, too, and I have to acknowledge that they not only confirm my story but also permit me to change it as I go along, creatively, into the future, adding elements whose fit into the gestalt can, over time, transform it drastically.

These elements are rigors. They amount to an ethical view of the world. Pretending avoids them. Pseudodepression is a failure to take up the rigors of life. It is a giving in to the ready-made story of being depressed, which tempts me to enact that story instead. Therapy for pseudodepression involves engaging one's own story vigorously. But that is not enough. We must also traverse the rigors of existential and essential guilt, which are the key therapeutic foci for agitated and pure depression.

Duplicity is the result of that double consciousness native to human beings. Its pre-reflective level is bound to the perceptual world but roams freely through it erotically and playfully. Its reflective, self-conscious level is heavily preoccupied with the themes of culture, including an ethical vision of the world. We are cultured creatures, and our behavior is cultured behavior, through the self-consciousness that is at once self-oriented and culturally patterned.

Some of the culture that we inhabit and that inhabits us is pathogenic, such as the availability of psychopathological characters as possible solutions to problems and ways of life. The duplicity that results from enacting them is pathological. In the case of pseudodepression, I do not live vigorously but rather merely give in to such a pattern. More drastically and importantly, some of that culture, such as pride, makes us vulnerable to losing the complexity of our duplicity and, hence, makes us vulnerable to getting drawn into the deadening orbit of essential guilt. Sincerity, like simplicity, is dangerous for creatures such as ourselves whose consciousness is doubled, but that doubleness not only creates problems for us, it is also the key to our surviving them.

Only humans see the option of an ethical vision of the world and experience at once the desire to affirm that vision and our incapability to live it without guilt. This "non-coincidence of man with himself," as Ricoeur has called it, motivates the production of myth, particularly those myths that deal with human evil. Through those myths, the rift or fault in human ontology becomes mediated, and life becomes livable. The agonizing and unrelenting realization of our culpability, as the results of human evil, pummels us with its ubiquity, gets accounted for, becomes comprehensible, becomes something we can grasp and claim and avow in the resolution to live well, to do good, to try, within our capability, to give more than we take from the moral stature of humankind.

But myths are not our only mediations. We struggle with our personal rift, our fault, through the creation of disciplines that study human evil and good, through institutions that attempt to deal with the same realities in the practical world, and through legal, economic, familial, political customs and laws that attempt to contain human evil and maximize human good. Each of these disciplines and institutions deals with the task of making life livable to a being who cannot escape noncoincidence with itself, the "disproportionality" between moral commitment and existential shortfall. These disciplines and institutions deal with the tasks by avowing the evil and the guilt, not disowning or denying it, but by saying in the premises of their own purposes that human beings must strive to overcome the gap, that participation in these institutions allows personal and collective hope for a future that is somehow better than our ever so checkered past.

Culture, all we've been talking about, has its place in my life in my second, cultured consciousness. My participation in culture is duplicitous with respect to the immediate world of my first consciousness, but that duplicity is absolutely necessary if I am to mediate my own disproportionality or participate in collective mediation as a way to do so.

Psychopathology is the disarray of that mediation. I sometimes follow patterns that are merely given in to, that are idiosyncratic and not cultural; my consciousness becomes disoriented amidst the pretendings. Amazingly, we work these things out eventually, often without help, even in the face of life's smaller and even larger insults. But when we do not, our narratives begin to show the signs of our per-

sonal rift; something does not fit, is no longer intelligible. A new mediation, a new narrative is necessary. Psychotherapy helps me to
reinterpret, indeed to reinvent, my narrative and, hence, myself.

If my pretendings have drawn me into the orbit of essential guilt, and
I stare into the face of human culpability, I am in danger of losing my
mediations, my culture, my duplicitous institutional loyalties and personal struggles to be a good person. I am in danger of giving in and giving up. To re-establish or reorder remnants of earlier duplicities is the
task of therapy. Part of therapy may display my real depression—not my
pretend depression or the sadness of loss, in the face of which I began
pretending, although that sadness will have to be lived through. In contrast to these is the depression of essential and existential guilt.

Such a route to my own story runs the risk of producing depression
where there was no depression before. But that is not a matter of mere
symptom substitution. The experiences of existential and essential guilt
are possibilities for tremendous personal growth. At this point, therapy
for pseudodepression and therapy for agitated and pure depression engage the same, further rigors.

Existential guilt puts one squarely in the role of author of my life
story. No one else did this or that, and no one else can add to what's
been done. My restitutions and expiations are additions to what I've
done. Such adding, of course, does not change what's been done, but it
does change the whole of which it is a part and, thus, it changes the
meaning of what's been done—its role in the narrative. An unattended
sin is not the same as one attended to.

Essential guilt puts my story squarely into a larger story of humankind, with its tragic flaws and its heroic courage. Such a sense of one's
own story (and identity) changes my perceptions of others as well as
myself. It changes the meaning of the failures of others and of the struggles and courage of others, and it yields forgiveness and respect. It also
confronts me with that sadness, much greater than my personal sadness, of human finitude and tragedy. This is humility.

These experiences can be transformative because they are not pretenses. They are, indeed, experiences of that border of human being at
which guilt and depression shape the Gestalt of human possibilities.
They are ontological experiences, after which the meanings of everything in our lives must change. The narratives we live take on a self-conscious depth and scope that transforms who we are.

If I can see my losses, my desires, my anxiety and my sadness in this
way, then my election of a path in a field of possibilities is a crucial
choice, a choice among alternatives as grand as heroism and cowardice

and as monumental as the definition of human nature. If I can see my choices this way, then I cannot be depressed.

Notes

CHAPTER 1

1. An extra layer or second consciousness, which is present in human beings and not (we suppose) in blue jays, is the capacity for human consciousness to focus reflectively back on itself, making the self and its consciousness into an object of one's own inspection. Sigmund Freud (1959) noted the importance of such self-consciousness in depression, and phenomenologists and other students of consciousness readily begin with the distinction between pre-reflective awareness and reflective self-consciousness. A compact phenomenological analysis of the distinction is contained in Richard Zaner's work (1970).

By all means, this concept of a second consciousness must not be confused with the occasional excitement in psychology about left-brain/right-brain consciousnesses, a distinction observable only in rare post-operative circumstances (Gazzaniga, Steen, and Volpe, 1979) and much too readily assimilated into our cultural distinctions between art and science, synthetic and analytic thought, and so on. I want particularly to distinguish this theory from Julian Jaynes's (1976) "bicameral mind."

2. I am indebted to Howard Pollio for the courage to begin this argument where it really ought to begin, with the distinction between reflective and pre-reflective consciousness. It was his book *Behavior and Existence* (1982), written for introductory students, that demonstrated that this starting point is possible without zooming off into the esoteric complexities of phenomenological philosophy.

CHAPTER 2

1. Clifford Geertz (1983) explains these points in some detail.

2. The naturalization of evil, the transformation, in our minds, of incomprehensible behavior, from mysterious events to supposedly natural and, therefore, comprehensible ones, is the modern version of something every culture does, namely, makes the incomprehensible comprehensible through assimilation into familiar categories.

As such metaphoric and/or mythic activities go, calling incomprehensible behavior "ill" rather than "possessed" or "demonic," moving it from mystery to nature, can be seen as a step toward more humanitarian concern, although it remains properly controversial (Szasz, 1970). But extending such naturalization to radically iconoclastic violence such as Nazism takes the phenomenon out of mystery, and the mystery out of the phenomenon, prematurely.

We do not understand Nazism, and our glib reduction of it to pseudo-explanations like metaphors of illness obscures what we should most squarely be facing: our own iconoclastic potentialities, including, of course, the lessened but continuing threat of the closure of history in thermonuclear war.

CHAPTER 3

1. Many authors have hinted at this concept of depression before me. The clearest is Willard Gaylin (1968) when he says:

We are conditioned to look for the "meaning of symptoms"; a meaning in terms of problem solving. Symptoms are attempts of the individual to compromise his way out of a conflict situation. They are the reparative maneuvers and manipulations of the threatened ego. In depression, however, the distinguishing feature is the paucity of such maneuvers. The "symptoms" are the non-symptoms of passivity, inactivity, resignation, and despair. Here the reparative mechanisms are at a minimum. The depressive is not like the phobic who had found an illusion of safety through the mechanisms of displacement and avoidance. He has no illusions. (390–91)

An explicit rejection of this view of depression by Gaylin is Greenacre (1953), who says:

It is . . . a positive, forceful affective state, thought in a negative direction, as in contrast to apathy or indifference which it may superficially simulate, and it implies inherently some degree of identification of the subject with the object lost. (8–9)

2. Kierkegaard (1941).

CHAPTER 4

1. My intellectual debts here are manifold. First, my historian friend and colleague, John Kirkland, first introduced me to the notion of narrative as the central vehicle of human meaning. Second, Alistair MacIntyre (1978) spelled

it out nicely. I have since also found it in the work of Julian Jaynes (1976) and Berne (1961), and also relatively early was Bruner (1986). Third, Theodore Sarbin's APA address in 1983, and then his edited volume (1986), *Narrative Psychology*, has done much to develop the concept in psychology.

2. It is important to see that what may have appeared to be a dichotomy between real and artificial depression becomes a more complicated theoretical structure when we take into account agitated depressions of various kinds. Instead of a "true" and a "false," there is a pure type, largely ideal—although nearly perfect versions can be found in any state hospital—and a series of approximations, some closer to the ideal type than others.

Like calling someone "good," there are degrees, and no one is perfect; and yet some are more good than others and we see those who, knowing the category and its attributes, try to appear to be good, or to become so by enacting it. And while the enactment may be a deception, or an effortful imitation, intentional or given in to, such enactments engage the actor in the essence which then proceeds to color who he or she is. This is also true of being really good; and it is true of being really depressed.

3. In a small town in Pennsylvania, a clinical friend of mine reports having treated in one year, concurrently, no fewer than ten anorexic patients. Most of them also claim to know several others, some of whom he does not know. Now epidemiology is a complex science. Common cultural, social, historical, and even geographical factors no doubt contribute to this epidemic of anorexia nervosa. But can we escape the conclusion also that "the anorexic" has become a character, one I can enact, and in doing so accrue certain psychological gains? Much is made, in such situations, of the relief felt when a patient discovers he or she is not alone in this strange way of life—as if they had never heard of the character. No doubt this happens, but we can, and should, also make something of the fact that anorexics often do know about the pattern of anorexia, its name, and often friends or acquaintances who offer concrete exemplars of the character.

CHAPTER 5

1. From Karl Abraham (1953, written in 1911) to Sigmund Freud (1959, written in 1917) to Sandor Rado (1928), depression has been seen by psychoanalysts as a version, a particularly pathological version, of mourning. Loss has, therefore, been in the center of the orthodox psychoanalytic interpretation of depression. Other unorthodox analysts too (Klein, 1964) also agree with this starting point. One must also mention a more current source, the American Psychiatric Association (1998).

2. Abraham, Freud, and other analysts also see anger as central to depression; specifically, guilt is anger turned inward in self-punishment.

3. See Glasser (1965).

4. See Seligman (1975), whose theory of helplessness extends to what is here called fear.

5. See Bibring (1953).

6. Since definitions are free, I am at liberty to redefine depression this way. The question is whether such a redefinition makes more sense than former definitions. Only the argument as a whole can answer that question, but I want to point out that such redefinitions are not uncommon.

After the psychoanalytic definitions were well established, Beck (1967) redefined depression in terms of a cognitive theory. Actually, Beck laboriously gathered data to develop criteria of depression and even a scale to measure it. Clinical judgments were used to know whom to include in the sample from which criteria were abstracted—a kind of democratic or naive realism strategy. Nevertheless, his theoretical treatment not only summarizes his data, it also tells him who should be included in his sample—or rather it tells his clinical judges—thus creating a circularity.

This is not illicit. The question is whether the model as a whole makes more sense than its predecessors. Seligman (1975) does the same thing in defining depression in terms of learned helplessness: "A laboratory model does not have the open-endedness of the clinical phenomenon; it clips the clinical concept off at the edges by imposing necessary features on it. So if our model of depression is valid, some phenomena formerly called depressions will probably be excluded." To be explicit, Seligman notes: "The label 'depression' applies to passive individuals who believe they cannot do anything to relieve their suffering, who become depressed when they lose an important source of nurture . . . but it also applies to agitated patients who make many active responses, and who become depressed with no obvious external cause" (1975, 93). Of course, depression is not one thing:

Learned helplessness need not characterize the whole spectrum of depressions, but only those primarily in which the individual is slow to initiate responses, believes himself to be powerless and helpless, and sees his future as bleak—which began as a reaction to having lost his control over gratification and relief from suffering. . . . The definition and categorization of illness is customarily refined by the verification of a theory about the illness. The presence of little poxes on the body was once the defining feature of smallpox. Then a germ theory of smallpox was proposed and confirmed, the presence of the germ became part of the definition. . . . As a result, some cases previously called smallpox were excluded, and others, previously ignored, were included. Ultimately, if the learned-helplessness model of depression proves adequate, the very concept of depression may be reshaped. . . . If learned helplessness significantly illuminates some depressions, others, such as manic-depression, may eventually be seen as a different disorder, and still other problems, such as the disaster syndrome, that are not usually thought of as depression, may be called depression. (1975, 93)

It should be noted that Seligman's view is neither static nor beyond dispute. See Abramson, Seligman, and Teasdale (1978), Costello (1978), and Depue and Monroe (1978).

7. For an elaboration of the notion of "strategic action," as an alternative to medical and deterministic theories so common in American psychology in the 20th century, see Sarbin and Keen (1998).

8. This technique may also be seen as a human extension of the common practice among competitors in the animal kingdom to surrender by exposing their vulnerability, thus provoking in the other an immediate cessation of hostilities. I am indebted for the Lenny Cohen story to Leonard Cohen, *The Favorite Game* (1963).

9. It is worth pointing out that persons who do not grow up in families are those most likely to be diagnosed psychopathic, or anti-social—indicating a lack of guilt. This would support Freud's theory—or perhaps merely reflect it.

There are, of course, many things to say about this definition of guilt. Notice that it is a certain kind of definition, one that describes the situation in which it is experienced (having hurt a person). Such a definition can be distinguished from an introspective one, which would perhaps analyze it into cognitive and affective components.

It is also distinct from an explanation of its origins in the language of causality, such as the developmental and instinctual language of Freud. Defining an emotion in terms of a situation has distinct virtues, pointed out by Buytendijk (1962) and Fell (1977).

Very briefly, we may say that such a definition says how I cognitively grasp a situation, how I feel, how my physiology responds and how my behavior inserts me into a situation—all at once, without separating these out for abstract consideration. Hence, fear is the emotion of a dangerous situation; anger is the emotion of a frustrating one, and so on. Defining emotions in terms of experiences of situations is defining them as part of one's being-in-the-world.

Guilt, then, is how one is when the situation involves having hurt another person. It is not a feeling, not merely mental, or a psychological phenomenon. It is a moral phenomenon. Morality is as basic to human being as mentality. Defining guilt this way prohibits the reduction of morality to psychology, which is so common in this century. As I shall show, it makes our dealing with ontology necessary.

10. The example of Nazi Germany in the 1930s and 1940s comes immediately to mind, and scholars have puzzled greatly over the presumed charisma of Hitler (Bullock, 1971), an interest that inspired re-publication of Heiden's (1944) effort as late as 1999 in English.

11. Defining guilt as ontological instead of psychological is common in Western theologies, and the psychological replacement of such definitions reflects the secularization and naturalization of nearly everything in the 20th century, particularly. As argued in note 2 of chapter 2, such demystification is premature, produces the illusion of understanding what we do not, and thus

mystifies our sense of evil, guilt, death, and pain after all. It is human, not Oedipal or Pavlovian, to feel guilt when I hurt another.

12. I emphasize again the importance of the moral content of the present theory. If depression comes from guilt, and guilt is a moral, not psychological (or not merely psychological) event, then depression is a moral event as well. Does that mean that those who are depressed are sinners and deserve to be depressed? Decidedly not, although the next chapter (see chapter 6) is needed to explain that point. In the meantime, it may be useful to contrast this view with one that clearly reduces morality to psychology. Seligman (1975), for example, points out:

In the last few years, many of my students have come to tell me that they felt depressed. Often they attributed their depression to their belief that life had no intrinsic meaning, that the Vietnam War would never end, that the poor and the black are oppressed, or that our leaders are corrupt. These are legitimate concerns. . . . But was the feeling, the actual depression, caused directly by these issues? Clearly, for a poor person, a black, or a student about to be drafted, these propositions could directly cause depression. But most of those I saw were neither poor, nor black, nor about to be drafted; these propositions were remote from their daily lives.

Here, Seligman's elaboration is crucial:

Yet they said they were depressed about them—not just concerned or angry, but depressed. To me, this meant that they were feeling bad about something much closer to home, bad about themselves, their capacities, and their daily lives. Such existential depressions are rampant today. . . . At first it seems paradoxical. More of the good things of life are available now than ever before: more sex, more records, more intellectual stimulation, more books, more buying power. On the other hand, there have always been wars, oppression, corruption, and absurdity; the human condition has been pretty stable along these lines. . . . Why should this particularly fortunate generation find itself especially depressed? I think the answer may lie in the lack of contingency between the actions of these students and the good things, as well as the negative events, that came their way. . . . These reinforcers came about less through the efforts of the young individuals who benefited from them, than because our society is affluent. They have experienced a minimum of hard work followed by reward. From where does one get a sense of power, worth, and self-esteem? (87–88)

Seligman's conclusion is decisive in refuting the notion that learning theory can explain guilt. For Seligman, human consciousness is sensitive to other origins of our morality: "Not from what he owns, but from long experience watching his own actions change the world" (1975, 88–89). He does not, however, tell us much about the morality he has in mind. Seligman's point is that guilt and depression are to be explained by the relationship (or lack thereof) between one's efforts and one's advantages. It is partly a matter of contingency, and, as he adds, a matter of one's current situation. But Seligman also fails to reach the moral issue, one's sense of justice.

A sense of justice does not reduce to contingency and is not a mere inference from a consciousness of one's unearned advantage, which in itself can, and often is, merely called good luck. A sense of injustice is explained by a morally sensitive perception of inequalities, unfairness, suffering and exploitation, not by amorally deaf and mute psychology. I, therefore, agree with Seligman that a sense of justice involves a sense of social realities, including inequalities, and so on. But the defining issue is not merely psychological; it is moral. Seligman never takes that theoretical step.

Before I move to psychopharmacology and the elimination of guilt, I should elaborate on guilt as inherent in human nature and explore further the strange disappearance of guilt during wartime.

One version of the experience of war is that of an athletic competition. To assimilate war into a team sport is to enable people to kill other people with no more remorse than to win on the playing field. Of course, war is more profoundly experienced because of the danger of losing one's own life, but not notably because of killing others. This killing of others is justified in the same way the scoring of points is justified: They want to do it to me, so I want to do it to them. This is competition; it is life and death, but life is like that. War is as natural as a competition on the playing field, and just as my loyalty to the home team must have no mercy for the feelings of the losers of the game, so must I have no empathic sense that war kills the enemy.

There are, of course, soldiers who suffer from guilt for killing the enemy. But this is rare. I remember a movie, inspired by World War II in the 1940s. This movie featured a prolonged sea battle between an American battleship and a German submarine and concluded with the fatally damaged submarine surfacing just before it sank. The captain of the battleship went to the deck and watched as the captain of the submarine also emerged atop the submarine. They saluted one another as the German ship sank beneath the waves.

We see here a touching moment. Military officers, mortal enemies, who have respect for one another across the gaping abyss of total war, who express this respect at the conclusion of the battle, dramatically expressed in the disappearance of the German captain beneath the water. What is the nature of this respect? Each recognizes that the other did what he had to do, given the circumstances. Had these two men met under different circumstances, they surely would not have enacted this scene, but the war context made the competition inevitable and final. Both were trained as fighting men, military officers for whom honor was more important than life.

This is an exaggeration of what I was taught as an athlete in high school, but not much. We knew that the contest was not final. We knew we would survive to live another day, perhaps to meet again. We also knew, however, that at the time of the contest, every ounce of energy, will, desire, and muscular skill was involved in the contest. However important it was to win—and it was as important in the life of my high school self as anything has ever been to me—it was even more important that at the end of the game, we were to be models of good sportsmanship, to be gentlemen who respected one another's skill, regardless of who won the game.

I recall wanting to win very much. I recall being made to feel that it mattered as much as anything in my life, at least for the time being. I recall being willing to take uncommon risks and sacrifices in order to win. Winning the game became everything; at the time of the game, the game became the whole of life. Nothing else mattered. Of course, my concentration could be disrupted by seeing my friends on the sidelines, but I was taught to focus, to ignore life in its usual dimensions and to dedicate my heart and soul to one task—to win.

The only greater context that mattered was that of sportsmanship. One had to do so honorably, to play by the rules, to be a gentleman, to win with honor, and if there was a disgrace greater than losing, it was to break those other, less focal, more marginal, but absolutely insuperable rules of sportsmanship.

CHAPTER 7

1. To the list of those who see modern morality as vestigial, I would add Nisbet (1975), Berger, Berger, and Kellner (1974), and Lasch (1979). B. F. Skinner (1971), of course, recommends leaving morality behind. In opposition to these fears and hopes about the demise of morality, academic philosophy has experienced a resurgent interest in morality along the lines of social justice. This wholesome discussion was begun by Rawls (1971) and taken up by Nozick (1974), Ackerman (1980), Walzer (1983), and others.

2. Ricoeur's philosophy is hardly easy to summarize, and yet I find myself so impressed by an underlying simplicity and obviousness that I shall try to do so. Philosophical language, not to mention the fact that I am working from a translation from the French, inevitably makes the formulations sound formal and stilted. Thus, I have taken considerable liberty in expressing Ricoeur's philosophy in English.

As a phenomenologist, Ricoeur's thought is very close to everyday human experience, and this is a help. But what he makes of these experiences involves concepts that are less intuitively obvious. Any line of thought that offers an interpretation of everyday experience different from that of the dominant culture is bound to constitute a challenge.

3. It is important at this point not to reduce imagination and transcendence to brain events, which we understand in terms of causality. Such a reduction will manifestly misunderstand them. They must be grasped, like beauty and goodness, intellectually, apart from the baggage of a scientific definition of reality and knowledge (such as reducing my imagination to brain events). The nonscientific framework within which we make these things intelligible must not be sacrificed if we are to function in clinical psychology or in psychiatry, or any human, value-laden enterprise apart from science.

4. An astonishing absence in modern psychological literature is a discussion of pride, or of morality as an agonizing choice between good and evil. Of course, modern secularization perhaps pushed us all away from religious concepts, but psychology can hardly justify not making pride, or good and evil, into an object of some intense study and reflection. I have found mention of pride in books by McDougall (1908) and Jules Henry (1973), and in philosophers such as Nietzsche (see *Genealogy of Morals*), but in general, this is a shocking omission.

5. Note at this point how close my formulation comes to that of Seligman (see note 10, chapter 5), a view I have disagreed with. The similarity of the views should not obscure the difference, which is that for Seligman these phenomena all occur in the neutral realm of nature, whereas I interpret them as belonging to the moral realm of culture.

Bibliography

Abraham, K. (1953). Notes on the psycho-analytical investigation and treatment of manic depressive insanity and allied conditions. *Selected Papers of Karl Abraham*. New York: Basic Books.

Abramson, L.Y., Seligman, M.P., and Teasdale, J.D. (1978). Learned helplessness in humans: Critique and reformulation. *Journal of Abnormal Psychology, 87,* 49–74.

Ackerman, B.A. (1980). *Social justice in the liberal state*. New Haven, CT: Yale University Press.

Akiskal, H.S. (1978). The nosological status of neurotic depression. *Archives of General Psychiatry, 35,* 756–766.

Allport, G.W. (1937). *Personality: A psychological interpretation*. New York: Holt.

American Medical Association. (1990). *Essential guide to depression*. New York: Pocket Books.

American Psychiatric Association. (1983). The bipolar spectrum: New concepts in classification and diagnosis. In Grinspoon, L. (Ed.). *Psychiatry update: The annual review*, vol. 2. Washington, DC: American Psychiatric Press.

———. (1994). *Diagnostic and statistical manual of mental disorders* (4th ed.). Washington, DC: American Psychiatric Association.

Andreasen, N.C., Grove, W.M., Maurer, R. (1980). Cluster analysis and the classification of depression. *British Journal of Psychiatry, 137,* 256–265.

Beck, A.T. (1967). *Depression*. New York: Hoeber.

Beck, A.T., Ruch, A.H., and Shaw, B.F., et al. (1979). *Cognitive therapy for depression.* New York: Guilford.

Berger, P., Berger, B., and Kellner, H. (1974). *The homeless mind: Modernization and consciousness.* New York: Vintage.

Berne, E. (1961). *Transactional analysis in psychotherapy.* New York: Grove Press.

Bibring, E. (1953). The mechanism of depression. In Greenacre, P. (Ed.). *Affective disorders.* New York: International Universities Press, pp. 14–47.

Breggin, P.R. (1991). *Toxic psychiatry: Why therapy, empathy, and love must replace the drugs, electroshock, and biochemical theories of the "new psychiatry."* New York: St. Martin's Press.

Bruner, J.S. (1966) *Toward a theory of instruction.* Cambridge, MA: The Belknap Press of Harvard University Press.

Bullock, A. (1971). *Hitler: A study in tyranny* (abridged ed.). New York: Harper-Perennial.

Buytendijk, F.J.J. (1962). The phenomenological approach to the problem of feelings and emotions. In Ruitenbeek, Hendrik (Ed.). *Psychoanalysis and existential philosophy.* New York: Dutton, pp. 155–178.

Cohen, L. (1963). *The favorite game.* New York: Viking.

Costello, C.G. (1978). A critical review of Seligman's laboratory experiments on learned helplessness and depression in humans. *Journal of Abnormal Psychology, 87,* 21–31.

Depue, R.A., and Monroe, S.M. (1978). Learned helplessness in the perspective of the depressive disorders. *Journal of Abnormal Psychology, 87,* 3–20.

Ellis, A. (1962). *Reason and emotion in psychotherapy.* New York: Lyle Stuart.

Erikson, E. (1958). *Young man Luther.* New York: Norton.

Fell, J.P. (1977). The phenomenological approach to emotion. In Candland, D.K., et al. (Eds.). *Emotion.* Monterey, CA: Brooks/Cole, pp. 254–285.

Freud, S. (1917, 1959). Mourning and melancholia. In *The collected papers of Sigmund Freud* (James Strachy, ed.) vol. IV. New York: Basic Books.

Gaylin, W. (1968). Epilogue. In Gaylin, W. (Ed.). *The meaning of despair.* New York: Science House, pp. 387–391.

Gazzaniga, M., Steen, S., and Volpe, B.T. (1979). *Functional neuroscience.* New York: Harper and Row.

Geertz, C. (1983). Common sense as a cultural system. In *Local knowledge.* New York: Basic Books, pp. 73–93.

Glasser, W. (1965). *Reality therapy.* New York: Harper and Row.

Goldfarb, A.I. (1975). Depression in the old and aged. In Flach, F., and Draghi, S.C. (Eds.). *The nature and treatment of depression,* New York: John Wiley & Sons.

Greenacre, P. (Ed.). (1953). *Affective disorders: Psychoanalytic contributions to their study.* New York: International Universities Press.

Healy, D. (1997). *The anti-depressant era.* Cambridge, MA: Harvard University Press.

Heiden, K. (1999). *The Fuehrer.* (trans. Ralph Manheim). New York: Carroll & Graf.

Henry, J. (1973). *Pathways to madness.* New York: Vintage.

Horney, K. (1950). *Neurosis and human growth.* New York: Norton.

Hull, C.L. (1943). *Principles of behavior.* New York: Appleton Century.

Illich, I. (1976). *Limits of medicine; Medical nemesis: The expropriation of health.* Baltimore, MD: Penguin.

James, W. (1890). *Principles of psychology.* New York: Holt.

Jaynes, J. (1976). *The origin of consciousness in the breakdown of the bicameral mind.* Boston: Houghton Mifflin.

Karasu, T.B. (1990). *Psychotherapy for depression.* Northvale, NJ: Jason Aronson.

Keen, E. (1984). Emerging from depression. *American Behavioral Scientist, 27,* 801–812.

———. (1998). *Drugs, therapy, and professional power.* Westport, CT: Praeger.

———. (2000a). *Chemicals for the mind: Pharmacology and human consciousness.* Westport, CT: Praeger.

———. (2000b) Emotional narratives: Depression as sadness; anxiety as fear. Paper in the symposium: Emotional life narratives: The good, the bad, and the creative. American Psychological Association Convention, Washington, D.C., August 8, 2000.

———. (2001). *A history of ideas in American psychology.* Westport, CT: Praeger.

Kekes. J. (1988). *The examined life.* Lewisburg, PA: Bucknell University Press.

Kelly, G. (1955). *The psychology of personal constructs* (2 vols.). New York: W. W. Norton.

Kierkegaard, S. (1941). *The sickness unto death.* Princeton, NJ: Princeton University Press.

Klein, M., and Riviere, J. (1964). *Love, hate and reparation.* New York: Norton.

Klerman, E.L., Weissman, M.M., and Rounsaville, B. J., et al. (1984). *Interpersonal psychotherapy for depression.* New York: Basic Books.

Kohlberg, L. (1963). Development of children's orientations toward a moral order. *Vita Humana, 6,* 11–36.

Lasch, C. (1979). *The culture of narcissism.* New York: Norton.

Lesse, S. (1974). *Masked depression.* New York: Jason Aronson.

Levinson, D. (1978). *The seasons of a man's life.* New York: Alfred A. Knopf.

McDougall, W. (1908, 1960). *An introduction to social psychology.* London: Methuen.

MacIntyre, A. (1978). The relationship of theory to narrative in social scientific understanding. A paper at the symposium, *Explanation and Understanding in the Social Sciences*. The College of Wooster, Wooster, Ohio, April 23, 1978.

———. (1981). *After virtue*. Notre Dame, IN: University of Notre Dame Press.

MacIver, R.M. (1957). Introduction. In Polanyi, Karl. (Ed.). *The great transformation*. Boston: Beacon Press.

Mirowsky, J., and Ross, C.E. (1989). *The social causes of psychological distress*. New York: Aldine de Gruyter.

Mowrer, O.H. (1967). *Morality and mental health*. Chicago: Rand McNally.

Nietzsche, F. (1968). Toward the geneology of morals. In *The basic writings of Nietzsche* (trans. Walter Kaufman), New York: Modern Library, 1968.

Nisbet, R. (1981). *Twilight of authority*. New York: Oxford University Press.

Nozick, R. (1974). *Anarchy, state, and utopia*. New York: Basic Books.

Perry, W. (1981). Cognitive and ethical growth: The making of meaning. In Chickering, A. (Ed.). *The modern American college*. San Francisco: Jossey-Bass.

Polanyi, Karl. (1957). *The great transformation*. Boston: Beacon Press.

Pollio, H. (1982). *Behavior and existence*. Monterey, CA: Brooks/Cole.

Rado, S. (1928). The problem of melancholia. *International Journal of Psychoanalysis, 9*, 420–438.

Rawls, J. (1971). *A theory of justice*. Cambridge, MA: Harvard University Press.

Ricoeur, P. (1965). *Fallible man: Philosophy of the will*. (trans. Charles Kelbley). Chicago: Henry Regnery.

Sarbin, T.R. (1986). The narrative as a root metaphor for psychology. In T. R. Sarbin (Ed.). *Narrative psychology: The storied nature of human conduct*. New York: Praeger.

———. (1993). The narrative as the root metaphor for contextualism. In S. Hayes, et al. *Varieties of scientific contextualism*. Reno, NV: Context Press.

———. (2000). Narratives of emotional life. In Sundararajan, L. et al. Emotional life-narratives: The good, the bad, the creative. American Psychological Association Symposium, August 8, 2000, Washington D.C.

Sarbin, T.R., and Keen, E. (1997). Sanity and madness: Conventional and unconventional narratives of emotional life. In Fack, W.F. (Ed.). *Emotions in psychopathology: Theory and research*. New York: Oxford University Press, pp. 130–146.

———. (1998). Nontraditional ways of classifying mental disorders. In Friedman, H S. (Ed.). *Encyclopedia of mental health*. San Diego, CA: Academic Press.

Scheff, T.J. (1975). *Labeling madness.* Englewood Cliffs, NJ: Prentice Hall.

Scheib, K.S. (1995). *Self studies: The psychology of self and identity.* Westport, CT: Praeger.

Scull, A. (1989). *Social order/Mental disorder. Anglo-American psychiatry in historical perspective.* Berkeley: University of California Press.

Seligman, M. (1975). *Helplessness: On depression, development, and death.* San Francisco: Freeman.

Skinner, B.F. (1971). *Beyond freedom and dignity.* New York: Bantam.

Spitz, R. (1965). *The first year of life.* New York: International Universities Press.

Szasz, T.S. (1961). *The myth of mental illness: Foundations of a theory of personal conduct.* New York: Hoeber/Harper.

———. (1970). *The manufacture of madness.* New York: Harper.

———. (1987). *Insanity: The idea and its consequences.* New York: Wiley.

Unger, R.M. (1975). *Knowledge and politics.* New York: Free Press.

U.S. Public Health Service. (1993). *Depression in primary care: Treatment of depression.* Washington, DC: AHCPR Publication No. 93–0551.

Valenstein, E.S. (1986). *Great and desperate cures: The rise and decline of psychosurgery and other radical treatments for mental illness.* New York: Basic Books.

Walzer, M. (1983). *Spheres of justice: A defense of pluralism and equality.* New York: Basic Books.

Weiner, I.B. (1975). Depression in adolescence. In Flach, F.F., and Draghi, S.C. (Eds.). *The nature and treatment of depression.* New York: Wiley.

Wiener, M. (1989). Psychosocial transactional analysis of psychopathology: Depression as an exemplar. *Clinical Psychology Review, 9,* 295–321.

Wilson, E.O. (1975). *Psychobiology: The new synthesis.* Cambridge, MA: Harvard University Press.

Zaner, R. (1970). *The way of phenomenology.* New York: Pegasus.

Name Index

Subject Index

giving up, 48–49, 53
group identity, 105
guilt, 49, 106; absence of, 66;
    angry, 102; essential, 99–100,
    105, 107–108, 111; existen-
    tial, 101, 106, 111; Freud's
    view of, 61–65; as a human
    given, 68–69; as the human
    situation, 70; inevitability of,
    93; Jewish mother technique,
    64; as ontological, 68; pre-
    tending, 102–103; and
    self-punishment, 66; and so-
    cial order, 62–64

happiness versus pleasure,
    95–96
hope, 80
human consciousness, nature of:
    finitude/infinitude, 93; free-
    dom, morality, fault, 90, 94;
    guilt, 90, 93, 110; limits, 52,
    101; memory, 90

individual cases versus universal-
    istic rules, 86–87
infinite in everyday life, 88–89

liberalism, 86
loss, 58

maturity, 67
medicalization, vii, ix, 76–79
morality, 85; and guilt feelings,
    85–86; as inevitable, 104; and
    ontology, 85–86; psychiatry
    as moral failure, 98; as vesti-
    gial, 87, 97
mourning, 41, 50
myths, 110

narrative, 41, 50, 106; collapse
    of, 105–106, 110–111; de-
    pressive, 54–55; engaging
    one's own, 51; of essential
    guilt, 101; falsifying of, 102
Nazism, 103, 105
nonbeing, 90

ontological: doubleness, 88; fal-
    sification, 105

past, clinging to, 31–33
pretending: and culture, 9; to be
    depressed, 35–37, 49, 52,
    100, 103; about the past and
    future, 31–35; purposeful, 21
pride, 48, 91, 100, 105; and de-
    pression, 93
psychoanalysis, 102
psychopharmacology, xv, 71–73;
    and the future, 74–75; in his-
    torical context, 72–75; and
    psychotherapy, 71, 72, 74

reduction of morality to psy-
    chology, 87
religion, 63

sadness, 80
self-concept, 105, 108–109
self-degradation, 102
self-discovery as recovery, 89
self-punishment, 102
sincerity, 1, 6
social order, authority and
    power, 63–64
spectrum disorder, xii
suicide, 102
survival of the fittest, 62

About the Author

ERNEST KEEN is Professor Emeritus of Psychology at Bucknell University. The author of numerous studies on aspects of psychology, his latest book is *History of Ideas in American Psychology* (Praeger, 2001).